Spanish Hours

Part memoir, part travelogue and part history, Simon Courtauld's book is a charming, idiosyncratic account of his love affair with this eternally fascinating country. In the tradition of classic English armchair travel writing, *Spanish Hours* is the perfect companion for those devotees of all things Spanish.

Spanish Hours goes to the heart of Spain and its people. It is about what matters in Spanish life, from fish to bulls, from monarchy to Gibraltar. The book also covers the dark forces which have always been at work in Spain, leading to the devastation of civil war in 1936. Memories of that war are never far beneath the surface in Spain, nearly every Spaniard has a relative who experienced it.

Simon Courtauld's wonderful book about his love for Spain and all things Spanish received glowing reviews when it was first published in 1997. He has revised the book and added a new chapter especially written for this paperback edition.

Simon Courtauld, born in 1940, was educated at Winchester and Trinity College, Cambridge, where he read law. During the many years he has travelled in Spain, he had also been legal correspondent of *The Times*, deputy editor of *The Spectator*, editor of *The Field* and a regular contributor to the *Daily Telegraph*. He is married, with two children, and lives in Wiltshire.

Elisabeth Luard is an internationally renowned cookery writer, artist and, recently, a best-selling novelist.

Spanish Hours

SIMON COURTAULD

Original illustrations by
Elisabeth Luard

LONDON

For Kim and Leila

First published in Great Britain in 1996 by
Libri Mundi

This revised edition with new material published in 1998

A catalogue record for this title is available
from the British Library.

ISBN 1 872037 04 6

Typeset by Antony Gray
Printed and bound in Great Britain by
MPG Ltd, Bodmin, Cornwall

Contents

Foreword

Madrid and Barcelona must be among the most stimulating of European cities – artistically, politically, journalistically – but they do not form part of this book. Nor do the questionable delights of the holiday resorts on the various *costas*. These are significant aspects of modern Spain; however, the characteristics of Spain and its people which I have tried to communicate are more enduring – as important decades, or centuries, ago as they are today.

In Spain, as in any country, there are certain things that matter. This book is the result of an attempt to understand those hours, or moments, in Spanish life (the word *horas* covers both) which go to the heart of the country.

While so many people have assisted me in small ways during my travels in Spain, I would like to thank especially: Vane Ivanovic for introducing me to bullfighting, Charlotte and Nick Scott for their frequent hospitality in the Sierra Morena, Alfonso Paz-Andrade for entertaining me at his house near Bayona, and Inigo de la Huerta at his family's estate near Oropesa. I am also grateful for their help to Javier Zarzalejos, Miguel Santiago, Teresa Maldonado and Mary-Jane Aladrin.

Most of all, however, I thank my wife Philippa for putting up with my many absences in Spain, and for sometimes accompanying me on the understanding (which I would somehow always overlook) that next time we would go to Italy.

In so far as I have drawn on articles of mine which have appeared in *The Spectator* and the *Sunday Telegraph*, thanks are due to the publishers.

ONE

By Way of Africa

Most people catch their first glimpse of Spain when crossing the Pyrenees at thirty thousand feet or arriving by car ferry on the industrial north coast. Initial impressions, if they leave any mark at all, will be misleading. My own first journey was unimaginative, by air to Madrid; it was not until quite recently that I drove across the frontier from Hendaye on the French south-west coast, and saw how strikingly evocative is the image of Spain that presents itself on the other side of the Bidassoa river mouth. The old walled town of Fuenterrabia stands upon a hill above the bay, dominated by a dark and forbidding church, which on closer inspection has blackened buttresses looking as though they had been scarred by war. The Daughters of the Cross reside next door in the Colegio San José. The power of the Catholic Church still seems unavoidable and all-embracing.

How many young Englishmen, I wondered, on their way to fight for Republican Spain in 1936, must have felt a chill of fear, and perhaps stopped in their tracks, as they looked across the Bidassoa and saw what they were up against. They were going not only to fight fascism but what both Franco and the Church called a Catholic crusade.

In fact this crossing to and from the Republic was not open for long: by early September 1936, less than two months after the rising, Fuenterrabia, together with the railway terminus of Irun, had fallen to the nationalists, and the escape route for Basques and Asturians to friendly France was closed. The stream of refugees fleeing across the frontier with their few possessions – by car, coach, horse, boat and on foot – soon ceased to flow.

A better organised march out of Spain had taken place in October 1813, when Wellington's army forded the Bidassoa here at low tide, guided by local fishermen. A painting by James Beadle shows the great commander, on Copenhagen, riding ashore on the French side and casting a final satisfied glance back at the town of Fuenterrabia and the country he was leaving victoriously behind.

Today the cobbled streets of the old town, the woman with her daughter begging for alms outside the Church of Nuestra Señora de la Asuncion, the originally eleventh-century palace which is now a *parador*, are quintessentially old Spanish. New Spain is most obviously represented by the lycra-shorted cyclists who ride from Fuenterrabia over the steep hill road of Mount Jaizkibel to San Sebastian.

Of the other routes into northern Spain – I have crossed the Pyrenees at several points on the way to the *feria* of San Fermin in Pamplona – the eastern end of the Pyrenees provides another, and quite different, contrast between the two countries, where a train takes you through a tunnel from the miserably down-at-heel border town of Cerbère to the rather more sprightly Port Bou on the Spanish side. To arrive in Barcelona by boat at dawn is impressive, but my stronger recollection is of a sense of early-morning confusion at the sight of a huge statue of Columbus surmounting a column nearly as tall as Nelson's. What was he doing in the capital of Catalonia, having made his great voyage from Andalusia, and why was he pointing towards the ancient rather than the new world?

To enter Spain by way of Gibraltar, because of continuing 'technical' problems, can be an interesting exercise. It used to be pleasant to take the ferry across the bay to Algeciras, but it has not run for the past twenty-five years. Long after the land frontier between Spain and Gibraltar reopened in 1985, disagreement continues over the sovereignty of the waters of the bay. Getting into Spain across the frontier to La Linea can be simple and painless, particularly on foot. But the Spanish authorities may decide, often over a hot summer's weekend, that cars should be delayed a little – which is especially frustrating for those British citizens who live in Spain but work on the Rock.

I used to think it fascinating to be able to walk from a quaint colony of uniformed British 'bobbies' and pubs with names like the Horseshoe, straight into a world of the Guardia Civil and *tapas* bars. But the Gibraltar government has behaved so obstructively in recent years, towards both Spain and Britain, that I feel almost embarrassed to arrive in Spain via this diminutive anachronism.

Much more instructive is to sail to Spain across the Straits of Gibraltar from Tangier, and remind oneself of the strength of the links with North Africa. It was in AD 711 that a Berber warrior, Tariq-ibn-Ziyad, landed with an army of seven thousand on the shores of southern Spain and within two years had conquered almost the whole of the Iberian peninsula.

Most place names in Andalusia derive from the Arabic; al-Andalus was the name originally given by the Moors to the whole of Spain. One wonders how many Englishmen know that Gibraltar (Jebel-al-Tariq) and Trafalgar (Tarif-al-Ghar) are named after Moorish invaders. Islam, of course, brought culture and learning to Spain, and there was a good measure of harmony between the Christians and their Moorish conquerors – and the Jews, whose persecution did not really begin until the fifteenth century.

The Mozarabs, while remaining Christian in occupied Spain, often wore Arabic dress and were bilingual. Even El Cid (from the Arabic *sidi* or lord), the legendary crusading figure credited with having inspired the rising against the infidel which was to lead to the reconquest of all Spain four centuries later, often dressed as an Arab and sang Arab songs. Moorish architecture was adopted and adapted both in secular and ecclesiastical buildings. In Toledo, the seat of the primate of Spain, the railway station hall was rebuilt in the 1920s in Mudejar style (with mosaic flooring and copper lanterns), while a Mozarabic Mass is still celebrated in the cathedral. (According to H. V. Morton, in *A Stranger in Spain*, many of the collects in the English Book of Common Prayer are straight translations from the Mozarabic.)

In spite of such enduring associations with its Muslim past, very little of Spain's eight centuries of Moorish history is taught in its schools. The period is often glossed over as 'the time of the gypsies' – which is insulting both to Moors and gypsies who, notwithstanding their similarly dark skins, have always remained rigidly separate. In 1992, when Spain celebrated the quincentenary of Columbus's voyage to the New World, which heralded a great Age of Discovery, there was a marked reluctance to acknowledge that 1492 was also the year in which the Catholic monarchs, Ferdinand and Isabella, finally expelled the Moors and Jews from Spain (which, like the conquistadors'

14

treatment of the Incas, would form part of what became known as the Black Legend). The victory of Christianity in Spain represented the beginning of the Age of Repression, some would say of a totalitarian state – in which the Inquisition ruled, heretics and homosexuals were burnt to death, Arab books were destroyed and gypsies were driven from the country.

There is not much more tolerance shown towards Muslims in Spain today. They, and the gypsies, are held largely responsible for the high crime rate in cities such as Seville and Barcelona. Nor, understandably enough, were the Moors popular with those Spaniards opposed to Franco. In 1934, when a miners' rising in Asturias had to be put down, Franco had no qualms about using Moroccan troops in the only region of Spain never to have been under Moorish occupation. Two years later, at the beginning of the Civil War, the *generalisimo*'s Christian crusade against the forces of darkness was supported by about seventy-five thousand Moroccans who, as part of the Army of Africa, provided the nationalists' most ruthless fighting force.

Los Moros were especially feared and reviled for their habit of castrating their victims' corpses, and to all republicans there was something deeply offensive about bringing them to fight in Spain. It was made worse by the fact that they took part in the capture of some of the old Moorish cities of Andalusia – Granada, Cordoba, Ronda and Malaga. To all republicans, and to some nationalists too, the suggestion of a sort of counter-Reconquista was unpalatable. So, after the war, was the fact that Franco kept his Moorish Guard (*Guardia Mora*) until 1956.

For much of Spain's history, the Moors had been the only foreign enemy, at whose hands the Spanish army suffered its most humiliating defeat at Annual in 1921, with the loss of some fifteen thousand soldiers and Spanish citizens. Not many years before, in 1895, at the end of another Moorish war, an envoy of the Sultan was struck in the face in a Madrid street by a Spanish general who resented a Muslim showing himself in the capital. Following a public apology, the cruiser *Reina Regente* was made available to take the envoy back to Tangier. To the distress of very few Spaniards the ship, which had not put to sea for some time, sank with all hands.

It is instructive to note the number of names which celebrate the violent deaths of Moors. The old patron saint of Spain was known as Santiago Matamoros (Kill-Moors); and I have come across more than one village called Matamoros (also one called Matajudios). There is a street in Talavera de la Reina, Calle Cabeza del Moro (Moor's Head), and the pass which divides Andalusia from New Castile is called Desfiladero de Despeñaperros, the Gorge of the Flinging Down of the (Moorish) Dogs.

Not surprisingly, a new wave of Moroccan immigration into Spain in the early 1990s was viewed with trepidation. They came in the night, aboard *pateras* (flat-bottomed boats) from harbours along the Moroccan coast. These illegal immigrants from the Maghreb were landed on remote beaches between Algeciras and Cadiz, and at the other end of Andalusia, near Almeria – in sparsely populated areas that are almost impossible to police after dark.

It was a relatively new problem. Before 1980 there was net emigration from the country and Moroccans came to Spain only in order to travel on to France or Italy. Moroccans entering Spain before 1991 were not required to have a visa. In that year, however, the situation began to get out of control. The government responded by permitting scores of thousands of Moroccans in Spain to legalise their status, while at the same time securing King Hassan's agreement to take measures to restrict the traffic across the Straits of Gibraltar and to help with the repatriation of illegal immigrants from other African countries who had entered Spain via Morocco. That was in 1992, since when Morocco has done little to stop its citizens from coming to Spain; nor will it take them back once they have arrived. In 1995 as many as fifty thousand were thought to have entered Spain illegally, to take their chance in a European community free of internal frontiers.

One of the problems is that, thanks to modern medicine, Morocco's population has nearly doubled in twenty years to more than twenty-eight million and is expected to reach thirty-five million by the end of the decade. If large-scale Moroccan immigration into Spain poses a threat for the future, so too does an influx of Algerians driven from their country by militant Islamists. The distance from Oran to

Almeria is little more than a hundred miles, and Spain's enclave of Melilla on the eastern Moroccan coast is very much nearer. Spain's other possession on Morocco's mainland, Ceuta, was so threatened in 1995 by Algerian and black African immigrants, especially from Rwanda, that a Brussels-funded 'security road', known as the Great Wall of Europe, was being built along the five miles of the Moroccan border with Ceuta, which is part of metropolitan Spain.

Ever since the first Moorish invasion in AD 711, Tarifa, which is the most southerly town in Europe, has kept its Muslim associations. Superficially these days, it may appear to be overrun by foreign windsurfers, but Tarifa is very different once you have passed through the rounded arches of the old town. There you come upon the white, flat-roofed houses with their dark-eyed inhabitants; and beyond the castle the Punta Marroqui stretches towards Africa. Rose Macaulay, travelling this way in 1948, wrote in *Fabled Shore* of the number of children who would follow and pester a lone foreign woman in the narrow streets of Tarifa – rather as they do in North African towns. My own, most abiding, memory of Tarifa is of the potent smell of oriental spices wafting from a bar where small, skewered kebabs, known as *pinchitos morunos*, were being grilled, perhaps by a man wearing a scarlet fez, over a charcoal fire.

I have also sniffed the smell of the East in a modern suburb of Granada, where in the Sunday morning market ground paprika, turmeric and coriander were being sold from large bowls lined up on trestle tables. Many of the stall-holders were North African Muslims or negroes, a few selling Moorish clothes, brasses and trinkets. Also in this market I saw rows of sacks containing dried herbs and flowers, each one labelled with the name of the condition – prostate, diabetes, haemorrhoids, arthritis, kidney-stones, varicose veins – which would be alleviated by an infusion of the mixtures in hot water.

In the far south of Spain, it is sometimes hard to believe that this is part of the European Union. While Spain continues to benefit financially from the Community, it will remain pro-Europe. But Spaniards do not take kindly to directives and regulations from Brussels. It may not be too fanciful to think that at least a part of Spain, rather than take orders from somewhere a long way north of the Pyrenees, may on occasion look longingly towards the African coast and reflect more sympathetically on its Moorish roots.

It was, after all, in Granada that the Nasrid dynasty was responsible for constructing one of the finest groups of buildings in the world. Nothing that has been written, or shown in illustrations and photographs, quite prepares you for the reality of the Alhambra. For my part, I found it more breathtaking than the Taj Mahal. The elaborate tile-work, the intricately patterned plaster carving, the honeycomb and stalactite ceilings, the *oratorio* in the Mexuar (recently restored) overlooking the Albaicin, the light and water in the patios, the backdrop of the high peaks of the Sierra Nevada – all are quite stunning. And, most remarkable of all, the Alhambra was built after the Moors had been driven out of the rest of Spain, during the two centuries when the kingdom of Granada was the last Moorish redoubt on the peninsula. Did its rulers suppose, one wonders, that they would survive for ever untouched within the tranquil beauty of their seemingly impregnable hill fortress? When the last king, Boabdil, was forced to leave the city in 1492, one can imagine the anguish with which he turned, going south into exile in the Alpujarras, for a last glimpse of this jewel in the Moorish crown. The place is called the Puerto del Suspiro del Moro, the Pass of the Moor's (Last) Sigh.

A small British community lived in a row of villas just below the Alhambra hill in the 1920s. Gerald Brenan, who was then living in the village of Yegen in the Alpujarras, recalls in *South from Granada* taking tea with the senior member of the British colony, Mrs Wood, 'a tall erect figure clad in a white linen dress that swept the ground, a high lace collar and a Leghorn hat'. He also writes of the Pension Matamoros, kept by a Scottish lady, Miss Laird – 'short, white-haired, always dressed in black'. When in Granada, Brenan would put up at one of the several inns or *posadas* in the Calle Alhondiga, which today is a shopping street – jewellery, children's clothes and a *corseteria* – with a sprinkling of dental clinics. On occasion he would walk the sixty miles back from Granada to Yegen; he once did it in a day, leaving the Calle Alhondiga at three o'clock in the morning.

Over the past seventy years the population of Granada has almost tripled. Parts of the modern city are typical of large conurbations

18

elsewhere in Spain. Almanjayar, a suburb on the northern outskirts of Granada, is a 1960s housing estate built to accommodate Andalusians who had migrated to the city from backward rural villages and some of the gypsy families who have traditionally lived in Granada. (Some two thousand gypsies still occupy the old cave dwellings on the hillside of Sacromonte.) Like other large residential urban developments elsewhere in Europe, Almanjayar consists principally of tenement blocks and wasteland, and has a high incidence of unemployment, drugs and violent crime. Scarcely a tree is to be seen, there has been no landscaping and dogs roam the rubbish-strewn waste ground. Washing lines hang on the dirt-brown walls of the buildings, which are also decorated with graffiti, one of them declaiming '*Judios No*'. From a second-floor window a woman was washing her car by throwing buckets of water on to its roof.

From the look of many of the residents, Moorish blood still seems to be running in their veins. Only five hundred years have passed since the end of Moorish rule in Granada; and Muslim life continued there long after the Catholic monarchs had conquered the city. Three years after Boabdil had departed, a German traveller, Hieronymus Munzer, recorded that in Granada he counted more than two hundred mosques, each with Moors praying inside, and in the evening he heard 'such crying from the towers of the mosques as can scarcely be imagined'. Most of the mosques, and the Muslim population, were concentrated in the quarter of Granada called Albaicin, a name which derives from the Arabic, Rabad-el-Bayyadzin, 'the place of the falconers'.

When Richard Ford went to the Alhambra in 1831, he described his impressions of Granada at night:

> Its lights sparkle like stars on the obscure Albaicin, as if we were looking down on the *cielo bajo*, or reversed firmament. The baying of a dog and the tinkling of a guitar, indicating life there, increase the fascination of the Alhambra. Then in proportion to the silence around does the fancy and the imagination become alive; the shadows of the cypresses on the walls assume the forms of the dusky Moor as, dressed in his silken robes, he comes to lament

over the profanation by the infidel, and the defilement by the unclean destroyer.

When I looked over the battlements of the Alhambra at dusk, I could hear dogs barking in the Albaicin, where the cypresses stood darkly against the fading whiteness of the buildings. No muezzins could be heard calling the faithful to prayer, but the atmosphere was unquestionably more Moorish than European. The walls of the Alhambra were tinged rose-red by the last light of the day; fires were being lit outside the gypsy caves of the Sacromonte; the distant hills were sharply etched against the evening sky; and bats were swooping over the Alcazaba.

TWO

From La Rabida to La Palma

One of the more instructive ways to see Spain would be by visiting its monasteries. One might start with La Rabida, in the extreme southwest near Huelva, where Columbus planned his voyage to America. He came to this little Franciscan monastery with his five-year-old son around 1484; the monks looked after the boy while for the next seven years he tried unsuccessfully to put his project before the Catholic monarchs, Ferdinand and Isabella. It was thanks to the intervention of one of the monks at La Rabida, Fray Juan Perez, that the Queen finally agreed to receive Columbus before the gates of Granada, and to grant his wish. Seven months later he sailed with three ships from Palos, just below the monastery.

Having taken Granada from the Moors in 1492 – the last Muslim king, Boabdil, surrendered and handed over the keys of the Alhambra on 2 January – Queen Isabella kept the vow she had made years before and founded a Franciscan monastery within the walls of the palace. It was built on the site of a mosque, with a chapel which retained some of the arches and decorative plasterwork of the original building; and it was here that the bodies of the Catholic monarchs were interred until the construction of Granada cathedral was completed in 1521. Part of a Moorish room is still visible today, within the courtyard of the monastery. It was abandoned by the monks in 1835 and converted to a *parador* in the 1940s.

The monastery at Yuste, in the foothills of the Sierra de Gredos, near

Plasencia, is no less famous, for having accommodated the Emperor Charles V for the last eighteen months of his life. Having abdicated in 1555 in favour of his son Philip, he was conveyed across the mountains in a litter, which can still be inspected at the monastery. There the Emperor lived simply, with a parrot and a cat, mending clocks and tending the garden, until he died crippled by gout. The monastery is now surrounded by tall eucalyptus, its gardens overgrown with comfrey.

Unlike Spain's churches, its monasteries are friendly rather than awesome places. One would not expect monks to be particularly concerned with temporal matters, but those I have met – unless they belonged to a silent order – seemed anxious to talk to visitors and interested to hear about their travels. In a monastery near Toledo, I once come across a monk, on a cloister bench, who was reading a Teach Yourself English book. When I asked him, in English, how long he had been studying the language, his reply, that he had been reading this book for about ten years, was delivered with such an excruciating accent that we decided to continue the conversation in Spanish.

In the Monasterio de Yuso, in the province of Logroño, I met a monk puffing at a cigarette who seemed delighted when he learnt that I was English, and not German as he had supposed. He expatiated with genuine admiration on the qualities of King Juan Carlos, who had opened a language school in the precincts of the monastery in 1992. Then he tried to sell me some wooden bookends carved with monkish figures, from a stall in the cloister; but I settled for a Coca Cola from a vending machine in the courtyard outside. A mile up the hill the tenth-century Monasterio de Suso was less commercial (only postcards on sale), but provided a sharp reminder of the macabre, which keeps cropping up in Spanish places of worship. There is little left in this building except for some horseshoe Moorish arches and, displayed behind glass in a niche set into a cave in the hillside, a monk's skull and a pile of bones.

It is well worth staying at a monastery wherever possible. At the Hospederia Nuestra Señora de Valvanera, high in the Riojan hills, dinner, which is served at 8.30 pm (unusually early for Spain), consisted of vegetable soup so thick you could stand a spoon in it, followed by fried eggs and *chorizo* sausage, with a bottle of red wine.

Circulating from table to table, a monk inquires about your journey while happily accepting a glass of wine. Like all good monks, they make their own liqueur (similar to yellow Chartreuse), a heady infusion of sweet cicely, camomile, and other herbs.

On the way up to Valvanera, through the steeply wooded hills of the Sierra de la Demanda, wild flowers – foxgloves, Lusitanian pinks, burnet roses, broom and great phalluses of Aaron's rod – are everywhere visible near the roadside, often growing out of rock fissures. Far below the River Najerilla ripples over stones. The road comes to an end at the monastery, which is overlooked only by mountains rising to two thousand metres and birds of prey raking the high tops. At the beginning of June smudges of snow still lay on the peaks. It is one of the most ravishing places in all of Spain.

Over a glass of the local *licor*, I looked up H. V. Morton's account of his stay at the monastery in the Estremaduran village of Guadalupe (ten Zurbarans in the sacristy), regretting that on my visit to Guadalupe I had stayed at the *parador* rather than the Hospederia del Real Monasterio. Morton reported that the gates of the monastery were locked at 10 pm, and that he sat at the window of his room watching the firework celebrations of Midsummer's Eve and listening to the dogs barking. I went out on to the parapet as the light faded, gazed up at the darkening silhouette of Mount Pancrudo and listened to the silence.

In the town of Najera, down the valley and back on to the main Logroño-Burgos road, an inscription on the red sandstone wall of the Benedictine monastery of Santa Maria la Real reads: 'The glorious achievements of the Spanish kings of the Reconquest live on in this Marian temple'. Visitors may be taken down to the crypt, where several of the early Spanish monarchs are interred. One can, almost literally, bury oneself in the past here; and it was quite a shock to return to the cloister to see a yellow building crane protruding against the blue sky above the monastery.

It is, of course, a cliché to talk of the clash of old and new. But it often came to mind, on my travels in northern Spain, when confronted by countless signs on the roads – most of them adorned with the European logo of twelve gold stars against a blue background – advertising the Camino do Santiago.

I suppose the Euro-connection can be justified by the fact that the two principal pilgrimage routes over the Pyrenees – from Roncevalles and via Toulouse to Jaca – formed a sort of bridge with the rest of Europe, bringing pilgrims, in medieval times, from France, Britain, Germany, Italy and Flanders. One may or may not like to look upon this as an early pioneering example of the move towards European union. It was certainly a movement of massive proportions that took place every summer to the shrine at Santiago de Compostela. 'He is no pilgrim who does not make his way to the tomb of St James and return therefrom,' wrote Dante in *La Vita Nuova*. The St James in

24

question was the son of Zebedee who, at some time before his martyrdom around AD 40, was supposed to have preached the gospel in Spain. It is surely legitimate to ask, therefore, why European Community signs are pointing the way to a shrine which commemorates a fisherman from the Sea of Galilee – who, according to scholarly opinion, probably never left Palestine.

During the early years of the pilgrimage, several monastic orders established hospices and priories for travellers along the route; but today's pilgrims, making their way by bicycle or car, have to put up at hostels or country inns. Few walk the full length of the five hundred-mile route, but one should not underestimate the significance of the pilgrimage, particularly to Spaniards. A few years ago the bullfighter Ortega Cano, having had a bad season, decided to take the road to Santiago, on foot, to find spiritual refreshment. The following year, when he returned to the ring, he fought like a man inspired.

Like any other pilgrim or heritage trails elsewhere in the world, the Camino de Santiago is in danger of becoming commercialised. I have yet to see ice-cream vans and drinks stalls by the roadside – or indeed any pilgrims' camp sites – but the proliferation of signs, some with huge maps of the region, soon becomes profoundly irritating. It is all very well to be informed where you are heading; but pilgrims to Santiago were, by the nature of their journey, adventurous people. They do not need to be nannied along the way.

On main roads the signs may occur every two or three miles – and not only when you are travelling in the direction of Santiago. It is rather endearingly Spanish to find the same signs, with their Euro-logos, for some miles on the road due north from Leon towards the Cordillera Cantabrica mountains and the coast. Santiago is, of course, due west of Leon; but one trusts that some business will be done by the innkeepers and restaurant owners on the northern road before the pilgrims realise they should turn left to resume a more direct route to their destination in Galicia.

Those modern pilgrims who want to arrive in Santiago on foot – with the emblem of St James, a scallop or cockle shell, attached to their rucksacks – but do not wish to overstretch their legs, may decide to put on their walking boots only for the last eighty or so miles, having driven or hitched a lift over the Piedrafita pass on the Leon-Lugo border. Once into the province of Lugo, the elemental aspects of Galicia soon become apparent. Finisterre (between Biscay and Sole on the shipping forecast) is at the region's western extremity, but long before you get to the 'end of the earth' the harshness of the countryside – grass and granite, small agricultural plots and usually foul weather – makes it easy to understand why it is often compared to the west of Ireland. *Café irlandes* is offered in restaurants, and also in this Celtic country you may hear bagpipes and dark tales of witchcraft. The people, too, seem to share with the Irish the same wily qualities; and there was no one more cunning, inscrutable or perverse than Galicia's most famous, if not favourite, son, General Franco.

The story goes that during Franco's last illness in 1975 he was talking to one of his ministers at El Pardo Palace when a noise was heard outside.

'What is that?' inquired Franco.

'It is your people, my general,' said the minister; 'they have come to say goodbye.'

'Oh,' said the *caudillo*; 'where are they going?'

Although probably apocryphal, the exchange neatly illustrates a trait of the Galician character that was especially pronounced in Franco. It is also said that when you meet a *gallego* (Galician) on the staircase, you cannot tell whether he is going up or down. But if, seventy-five years ago, you had met one with a suitcase in Vigo, you could be pretty certain that he was off to the New World. As the Irish emigrated to the United States to escape the misery and deprivation of life at home, so did the Galicians take ship for Latin and South America. There are more *gallegos* in Buenos Aires, or so they say, than there are in Galicia. In more recent years Galicia has provided large numbers of migrant workers in Germany, Switzerland, and to a lesser extent in Britain. However, the emigration figures are much lower these days.

It is not at first easy to understand why this should be so. Neither the economic prospects, nor the climate, seem to have improved; and the provinces of Lugo and Orense have the highest suicide rates, and some of the lowest per capita incomes, in Spain. The shipbuilding industry is in possibly terminal decline, the naval base at El Ferrol has been much reduced, and the agricultural population (which represented about forty per cent of the Galician workforce in 1980) is said to have been halved since Spain joined the European Community in 1986. Unemployment stands at twenty-five per cent, rather higher than the national average.

Yet things in Spain are seldom quite as they seem. If statistics are in general unreliable, in Galicia they tell a good deal less than half the story. A more interesting indicator of Galicia's economic life is the statistic – unofficial, of course, and possibly inaccurate – that there are more Mercedes cars registered in the province of Lugo than anywhere else in Spain. This is the visible face of the black economy. Galicia has an 'industry without factories': leather shoes, designer clothes (Galicia has some very good designers) and fur coats are made up in the back rooms of houses and destined for the wealthy markets of Madrid and Barcelona.

And then there are the drugs. Much of the cocaine and heroin imported, through the Colombian network, into Spain is brought by boat up the narrow *rías* (estuarial inlets of the Corunna and Pontevedra coastline where the locals dig for shellfish in the mud at low tide). The former tobacco smuggling mafias of Galicia have now turned, much more profitably, to drugs. I was told that a schoolgirl in the coastal town of Cambados, asked by her teacher what was her father's occupation, had replied without embarrassment, *'contrabandista'*.

No need to emigrate any more, one might think, when such rich pickings are to be had on the doorstep. There is also the question of a new Galician identity, if not nationalism – autonomy for Galicia was formally recognised in 1981 – which keeps many at home. There are television and radio stations in the Galician language, which is spoken by around eighty per cent of the people, though it is not a political issue. While the regional government is controlled by the right-wing Partido Popular (PP), with one of Franco's ministers, Manuel Fraga, still its leader in 1997 (he founded the PP's predecessor, Alianza Popular, in 1976), the nationalist party (Bloque Nacionalista Gallego) is increasing its support. There has even been an occasional bomb, the responsibility of a body calling itself the Union de Poder Gallego. But

27

Galicia is not expecting much more political tension or violence: unlike the Basque country and Catalonia, it has few industrial workers or immigrants, the most likely fomenters of trouble.

But the region still has, *pace* the statistics, a lot of farmers. Ministry of Agriculture surveys may show that the number of people in Galicia employed on the land has fallen sharply in the past ten years – and that the principal crops are now kiwi fruit, chestnuts, mushrooms and organically grown produce, in addition to beef farming – but that is not really the point.

The minifundia system still obtains in much of Galicia: it consists of 'handkerchief plots' of an acre or less, growing potatoes, kale and maize which, unless sold through a cooperative, may be carried to the local market, often on the head of an elderly woman. This 'survival' agriculture does not show up on the official statistics, whether for output or employment, but it continues in some areas largely un-changed since the system of tenure for smallholdings was established to cope with over-population several centuries ago. Some of the accommodation also seems to date back to this time: within the past few years there were families living with their animals in *pallozas* – thatched huts with granite walls. Many of the old cottages, however, have been abandoned and returning emigrants from Germany and Switzerland have built chalet-style bungalows, without any apparent planning restrictions or any thought for the landscape. Ironically, the same sort of thing has happened in Ireland, with bungalows con-structed in *hacienda* style, and often in garish colours, standing out hideously against the hillside.

The tiny plots of land in Galicia are usually separated by stone walls made from slabs of granite standing in line like headstones in a crowded graveyard. Oxen may be used for ploughing and a sickle for cutting the hay. An old lady with her house cow, on a long rope attached to its horns, will not be far away – walking it along the road or waiting while it grazes the verges. She will probably be dressed in black, with a black headscarf, and wearing *zuecos* (wooden clogs) or – since it is highly likely to be raining – she may be carrying an umbrella and wearing gumboots.

It was raining, and snowing, in December 1808 when Sir John

Moore's army was retreating through Galicia to Corunna, struggling over steeply wooded hills and across moorland covered with broom and gorse and blasted by the icy wind. (The Spanish weather, which is by no means always as clement as foreign tourists expect it to be, also played a significant role at the battle of Teruel in the civil war, during the extreme winter of 1937–8. On some days more lives were lost in the snow, due to frostbite, than as a result of fighting between republicans and nationalists.)

Above the harbour of Corunna, next to a military hospital, Moore's grave is to be found in a garden behind the ramparts – remembering the first lines of Charles Wolfe's poem – to which they hurried his corse. It is a suitably English setting: the garden is laid out with geraniums, lilies, hydrangeas and bushes of rosemary. Surrounding the cemetery and giving it shade, four beech trees stand sentinel, and a few of Wolfe's lines on the burial are inscribed on a plaque. In dedication to Moore, the Galician poet, Rosalia de Castro, wrote in 1871:

Please God, noble foreigner, that this be not an alien place for you. There is no poet or spirit of imagination that cannot but contemplate in autumn the sea of yellowing leaves which covers your tomb with love, or the fresh buddings of May . . . and say, 'How I wish that when I die, I could sleep in this garden of flowers.'

Visiting Moore's grave set me thinking of other English connections with Galicia. The aspect of the country and the weather do not draw British visitors these days – I have seen very few foreigners here, other than in Santiago – but they used to come, and not just as pilgrims. John of Gaunt invaded these parts in the Middle Ages, and Sir Francis Drake raided the Galician ports in the sixteenth century, to teach the Spaniards a lesson after the Armada.

It was from Corunna that Philip II embarked for England to marry Mary Tudor and, thirty-four years later, his Armada set sail on its ill-fated venture. Two hundred years later, the English navy made several unsuccessful attempts to seize the port of El Ferrol, of which William Pitt said: 'If England had a port like this, she would plate it with an armour of silver.'

Situated at the head of a long and sinuous estuary, about ten miles from the sea, the walled town of El Ferrol is even more famous (at least in Spain) as the birthplace of Franco and was given the appendage of 'del Caudillo', which was dropped after his death. A few years later, one of the last unreconstructed *franquistas*, Colonel Antonio Tejero, was imprisoned there for trying to overthrow the still fairly recently elected democratic government. Many will recall the television pictures of the almost burlesque figures of the Guardia Civil colonel and his men, wearing their tricorn hats, as they seized the parliament building in Madrid and held its members hostage for most of the night of 23 February 1981. Though the coup was quickly frustrated, by the intervention of the King, the spectre of military dictatorship, even of civil war, did return to haunt the Spanish people for a few dramatic hours. It was therefore quite a surprise to learn, three months later, that the man who had almost single-handedly held the country to ransom, although in prison awaiting trial, was not subject to the same restrictions as other people in custody.

In the summer of 1981, Tejero was being held in an old castle called La Palma, which stands on a promontory at the point of a narrow channel halfway between El Ferrol and the open sea. However, his conditions of imprisonment were anything but harsh. He was allowed to receive almost as many visitors as he wished, though officially limited to five a day; they were mostly officers of the army and his own Guardia Civil, sometimes with their wives, and an occasional journalist. Tejero had written an article defending his patriotism for the monarchist newspaper, *ABC*, and was suing another for having compared his action with ETA terrorism.

I was passing through Santiago at this time, and the local correspondent of *El Pais* suggested that I should go and see the colonel. I thought he was joking, but when he told me of the lax regime at La Palma and the number of people who had visited Tejero, I telephoned the prison. Would the colonel be willing to talk to a correspondent of *The Spectator*, a right-wing (carefully emphasised) English journal? I was asked to wait while he was consulted. The reply came back that Colonel Tejero was very busy, but that he would try and fit me in one day the following week. I regret to report that I decided not to wait that long.

Why was a man who, at the point of a gun, had threatened the democratic future of Spain, allowed to reside in relative comfort, in the birthplace of his mentor, General Franco, and communicate with officers who might well try to organise both his escape and another attempted *coup d'état*?

Part of the answer may have been that, in 1981, power and influence in the army and the Guardia Civil still remained largely in the hands of men who were loyal to Franco's memory. Of course Tejero had to be jailed, but the circumstances and conditions of his detention were out of the government's hands.

In the aftermath of armed rebellion in the capital, it was no doubt deemed prudent to remove him from Madrid and hope he might be forgotten in faraway Galicia. A sage, shoulder-shrugging and none too logical Spaniard might comment that there was nothing provocative about the Franco connection with El Ferrol; it was also the birthplace of Pablo Iglesias, founder of Spanish socialism. And after all, he would say, the colonel was a rather absurd tragi-comic figure, who could be indulged a bit. A few chats with his cronies, a bit of favourable newspaper publicity, were not going to lead to another conspiracy against the state – because the circumstances of his failure to take over the government ensured that democracy would not be threatened again. This may be an example of curious Spanish thinking, but it has proved to be right.

THREE

Black Nights

'Black is Black', produced in the early 1960s by a group called Los Bravos, was the first Spanish pop-song to get into the international charts. There was nothing very remarkable about the title – I certainly don't remember its context – but it stuck in my mind because of the colour. Black is not only black – black is also Spain.

España Negra is a term which it may be hard for a foreigner to understand. It is intrinsic to Spanish life and culture, it is deeply ingrained in the Spanish psyche, and it relates to unmodernised Spain. It is about passion and poverty and violence and despair (unforgettably depicted in Goya's *pinturas negras*). *España Negra* embraces bullfighting and the ceremonial killings of other animals, the half-pagan, half-Christian elements of village fiestas, and the wearing of black clothes by old women in rural areas. It is about tradition and ritual and the power of the Church. As recently as 1973, a Spanish tourist board poster showed four figures, hooded and cloaked in black, against the background of a windmill. *España Oculta*, it might also be called, which is the name given to the striking collection of photographs by Cristina Garcia Rodero (published by Lunwerg Editores, Barcelona) to illustrate some of these aspects of Spanish life.

Literary manifestations of *España Negra* go back at least as far as the sixteenth century and the early picaresque novels. The eponymous narrator in *Lazarillo de Tormes*, a boy who accompanies a blind beggar on his travels, takes his revenge on the old man for having denied him

32

food. At Lazarillo's urging, he jumps over a ditch and splits his head open on a stone post. Miguel Delibes and the Nobel prize-winning Camilo José Cela were among those writing during the Franco years about the harshnesses of more modern rural life. Black thoughts and deeds seem always to be present in *The Family of Pascal Duarte*, set in the poor village of Torremejia in remote Estremadura, in which Pascal kills, among others, his mother, his wife and his dog. Dark strains of anarchism and nihilism also run through this novel.

Both in literature and in life, the villages of south-west Spain seem to have exhibited the cruelty associated with *España Negra*. Lope de Vega wrote a play around Fuenteovejuna, a village in the Sierra Morena, in which the inhabitants, having killed their *cacique*, refused to say who was responsible. Even under torture, the only answer to the question, 'Who killed your chief?' was 'Fuenteovejuna'. A not dissimilar act of collective responsibility actually occurred four centuries later, in the isolated Estremaduran village of Castilblanco, south of Guadalupe. In this *pueblo* of nine hundred inhabitants, on the last day of 1931, the four-man Guardia Civil tried to break up a meeting in the village square, held to protest against high unemployment. Strikes were taking place all over the province, and there was much talk of agrarian reform. Feelings were running high among the *campesinos* of Castilblanco when the Guardia Civil, always unpopular and often brutal in their methods, decided to employ some physical force to clear the crowd from the square. In the resulting clash the four policemen were killed, their eyes were gouged out and thirty-seven knife wounds were counted on one body. It was said that the women of the village, in a macabrely primitive scene, then danced round the mutilated bodies. Castilblanco was taking its collective revenge on authority: it was murder by the community rather than a few homicidal individuals, though six were later to be sentenced to life imprisonment.

A year later, an anarchist rising at Casas Viejas, a miserable hamlet in a malarial region not far from Jerez, was led by a man nicknamed 'Seisdedos' (Six Fingers) who attempted an old-fashioned declaration of village independence. He and his followers were besieged by assault guards who set fire to the anarchists' house, killing twenty-five people. The reputation of the republican government of Manuel Azaña was dealt a severe blow by the Casas Viejas incident, leading indirectly to its defeat later that year. The right-wing government which replaced it ruled for two years which the Left, fearing a return to the past, called the *Bienio Negro*.

But it was not as black as the civil war that followed, which in its early months unleashed a spate of village atrocities and family vendettas. (Such vendettas, with the members of one family murdering another, have persisted until the present day – in the poor suburbs of large cities as well as in remote villages like Puerto Hurraco, in the province of Badajoz, where a notorious family killing took place in the 1980s.)

The civil war also fostered the revival of the Black Legend, which had its origins in the conquest of the New World, the expulsion of the Moors and Jews, and the campaign against Flanders. These were glorious episodes in Spain's imperial history – or they were unjust, shameful and cruel. The Legend grew thanks to a Dominican monk, Bartolomé de las Casas, who wrote scathingly of the conquistadors' excesses in *La Destruccion de las Indias*, which was translated and widely read throughout Europe. Though not written until much later, Verdi's magnificent opera *Don Carlos* helped the Legend along by portraying Carlos as the hero in his struggle on behalf of the Flemish heretics and against his father, King Philip II, and by its memorable depictions of the cruelty of the Inquisition and the omnipotence of the Grand Inquisitor. Spaniards were sensitive to this 'propagandist' view of their history with which other European powers had been, they would say, brainwashed. The Legend would be resurrected at various periods, to discredit Spain in the eyes of 'civilised' Europe, not least during Franco's time, when he would dismiss it as a conspiracy of communists and freemasons. Since Franco likened the civil war to a religious crusade against the forces of darkness, akin to the conquest of the Americas and the Christian defeat of the infidel Moor, it was hardly surprising that the Black Legend should be invoked against him.

In 1992, at the time of the celebration of the quincentenary of Columbus's discovery of the New World, it was noticeable that no mention was made of the other historic 1492 anniversary – the expulsion of the Moors and Jews from Spain. It may be that Spaniards have now expunged the Black Legend of the conquest of the Americas from their collective consciousness; but they still feel the need to explain to themselves the Legend as it relates to their ethnic cleansing of Muslims and Jews.

About other periods of their history they also have reason to feel unhappy. Seventeenth-century Spain, inward-looking and in decline, is best forgotten; and though the eighteenth was a century of reconstruction and, to some extent, enlightenment, the Bourbon dynasty did nothing to restore the position which Spain had held in the sixteenth century. After the disruption caused by Napoleon, and the French occupation of the peninsula, Spain stumbled through a century of disorder and strife which, it could be said, did not end until 1939.

When Franco railed against the nineteenth century, saying that it should be erased from the Spanish mind, he was of course referring to its liberalism. The 1812 Constitution of Cadiz established the party system, the right to vote of all male citizens, the equality of all people before the law and freedom of expression. To make matters worse in Franco's eyes, liberalism was associated with freemasonry and was anti-clerical. In the Church catechism (republished in 1927) the questions are asked: 'What kind of sin is Liberalism?' – 'It is a most grievous sin against faith.' 'Why?' – 'Because it consists in a collection of heresies condemned by the Church.'

It was ironic that the various nineteenth-century *pronunciamientos*, or military revolts, originally involved relatively few conspirators and were in support of the liberal revolution; whereas after the turn of the century the 'pronouncements' were for military dictatorship and, ultimately, for civil war against the Second Republic. Jan Morris has calculated that forty-three *coups d'état* were made between 1814 and 1923.

The civil wars of the nineteenth century set Liberalism against Carlism and town against country in much of northern and eastern Spain. Ferocious fighting continued for seven years, with priests often leading troops in defence of autocratic Carlism, which still had its supporters at the end of the century. Violence and revolution became a habit during these decades: a famous remark attributed to one of the country's many dictators, General Narvaez, is symptomatic of the time. When on his deathbed, he was asked by the priest, 'Does your excellency forgive your enemies?' To which the general replied, 'I have no enemies; I have had them all shot.'

When this disastrous century came officially to its end, the Spanish-American war had just resulted, in 1898, in the loss by Spain of its last important colonial possessions – Cuba, Puerto Rico and the Philippines. This led to the forming, by a group of radical intellectuals, of the Generation of '98, with the idea of determining how best to reverse the decline and regenerate Spanish society. In the simplest terms, opinion divided between the Miguel de Unamuno faction, academics and writers born around 1865–70, and the young essayist, José Ortega y Gasset, who was only seventeen at the turn of the century. Unamuno was for returning to the essentially quixotic Spanish values of the past, and to early nineteenth-century liberal ideas, while Ortega insisted on a break with the past. Spain had been Spain's problem, he said, and it required a modern European solution, founded in European socialism, science and culture. Unamuno and his literary contemporaries were searching the roots of Spanish culture for the spiritual soul of Spain, while Ortega envisaged a national revival through the integration of Spanish intellectual life into the mainstream of European culture.

One might ask how significant were these philosophical ideas, expressed in debates and essays which poured forth during the first three decades of the twentieth century, at a time when Spain was lurching inexorably towards the catastrophe of civil war. Spaniards love such debates: they may have profited from them, they may have derived hope from them. But the Generation of '98 did nothing, any more than did a group of poets calling themselves the Generation of '27, to alter the course of political events.

Ortega got very excited, after the end of General Primo de Rivera's dictatorship, at the prospect of a republic to replace the monarchy. 'The Republic means nothing less than the possibility of nationalising the public power,' he wrote; 'of fusing it with the nation, so that our people can devote themselves freely to their destiny . . . so that they can live according to their own ways and according to their internal inspiration.' Fine words, but within a year he had become disillusioned and had withdrawn from all political activity. '*No es esto*,' he said, 'it is not for this that we worked in the days of the monarchy,' commenting on the brutal repression, blamed on the government, of the anarchist takeover in Casas Viejas. What these intellectuals failed to understand was that their generation was no more than a hangover from the nineteenth century; the old Spain, with its separate classes and separatist tendencies, was not yet dead, and it was leading to revolution and revenge. One cannot avoid the conclusion that Ortega believed too implicitly in the truth of ideas. He was fiddling with philosophy while Spain was about to burn. When war came, he was so shocked by the atrocities and the influence of communism that he fled the country.

Ortega had never really understood the revolutionary nature of the politics which he sought to influence. Nor did he appreciate – perhaps because he was not a Catalan – the strength of anarchism in Spain. Although a few members of the Generation of '98 had flirted with the ideas of Michael Bakunin (the Russian aristocrat and founding father of Spanish anarchism), the anarchists distanced themselves from all bourgeois intellectuals, and after the founding of the Confederacion Nacional de Trabajo (CNT) in Barcelona in 1911, anarchism was essentially a syndicalist movement. It was an Italian, Giuseppe Fanelli, who introduced Bakunin's philosophy to Spain, in 1869; and a Catalan, Pi y Margall, who wrote influential tracts, around the same time, on the iniquity of the power of the state. Though at first strong in Andalusia, anarchism was suppressed there and moved on to take root in Catalonia.

For the last thirty years of the century Spain's political history becomes almost comical in its confusion. Amadeo of Savoy, Duke of Aosta, became King of Spain for about two years; Carlism enjoyed a brief revival; and the anarchist thinker, Pi y Margall, was elected president, for three months, in the 1873 republic. After a *pronunciamiento* had restored the Bourbon monarchy, Conservative and Liberal ministries, headed by Cánovas and Sagasta, alternated quite satisfactorily for about twenty years until 1897, when Cánovas was assassinated by an anarchist sympathiser.

Anarchism had by now migrated from the labourers of rural Andalusia (among whom was a revolutionary secret society known as *Mano Negra*, or Black Hand) to the workers of Catalonia and, more particularly, Barcelona. Bomb-throwing became commonplace – twenty-one people were killed at the Liceo theatre – as did police brutality in attempting to suppress it. European liberal opinion protested against the executions and the systematic torture in Barcelona's prison fortress of Montjuich, exhuming memories of the Inquisition and helping to perpetuate the Black Legend of Spain. One of the torture victims was taken round Europe to show off his mutilated body. The cycle of violence and repression finally culminated in the 'Tragic Week' of July 1909 in Barcelona, when a general strike degenerated into an orgy of destruction. Scores of churches and convents were burnt, nuns raped, graves dug up, and anarchist workers dressed themselves in stolen vestments.

The violence of anarchism, directed especially against the Church, continued during the twentieth century, got worse after the Second Republic was declared in 1931, and reached its height in the early months of the civil war. The persistence of this primitive anti-clericalism into the 1930s is one of the most signal facets of recent Spanish history. As Gerald Brenan puts it in *The Spanish Labyrinth*, to anarchists and libertarians the Catholic Church was more than an obstacle to revolution. It was 'the fountain of all evil, the corruptor of youth with its vile doctrine of original sin, the blasphemer against nature'. Such a persecution of religion, he wrote, had not been known in Europe since the Thirty Years' War.

It would be quite wrong to suppose that anarchists were a bunch of atheists. They wanted to destroy the Church not because it enshrined the Christian faith but because it was thought to serve only the interests of the rich. 'The anger of the Spanish anarchists against the Church,' Brenan wrote, 'is the anger of an intensely religious people who feel they have been deserted and deceived.' (Many of them would have read the teachings of Jesus in the New Testament, thanks to George Borrow's mid-nineteenth-century travels, particularly in Andalusia, on behalf of the British Bible Society.) There was in fact a religious and moral fervour about anarchism which distinguished it from Marxism and which accounted in part for the ferocious killing of priests and burning of churches in 1936. It was also said that anarchists feared the 'black magic' of the Church.

Well before the 1930s, the Catholic Church had begun to lose its hold on the Spanish people. Civil marriages and funerals were becoming common, and the vast majority never attended Mass or confession after leaving school. In some areas male attendance at church was no more than one per cent of the population of the parish, and around forty per cent would die without receiving the sacraments.

When anarchism threatened the Church's influence rather more directly, the response was scarcely less fanatical. The hatred between anarchists and the Church was entirely mutual, and there was certainly nothing irenic about the attitude of the hierarchy of the Church in Spain.

From the time of the civil wars of the nineteenth century, the Carlist followers of the brother of Ferdinand VII were committed to restoring the Inquisition; and it remained part of their programme into this century. In 1936 the Bishop of Badajoz spoke of rebuilding the Spain of Ferdinand and Isabella and using 'the cross and the sword together [to] return glory to our native land'. To the Catholic priesthood this was a holy war, a crusade, against republicanism, liberalism and socialism, but most of all against anarchism. Addressing the supporters of the rebellion, the arch-priest of Burgos told his congregation during Mass: 'You who call yourselves Christians show no mercy on the destroyers of churches and murderers of priests. May their seed be trampled under foot – for it is the evil seed, the Devil's seed.'

At least one instance is recorded of a priest unsuccessfully urging his villagers to put a number of Protestant evangelists to death. Where atrocities were committed against republicans in Andalusian villages, the local priests would intervene only to offer to hear their confessions before they were shot. It was very rare for a cleric's voice to be raised against the number of executions taking place. Regardless of the fact that fascist Germany and Italy joined Franco's forces, and that Moorish troops fought alongside Christians for the rebel nationalist army, both the Vatican and the Spanish Church gave them unstinting support throughout the war. The name of the Falangist leader, José Antonio Primo de Rivera, was painted or carved on the walls of every church. At the end of the war, Pope Pius XII wrote to Franco: 'Lifting our hearts to God, we give sincere thanks with your Excellency for the victory of Catholic Spain.' It was not until the 1960s that the Spanish clergy started to question Franco's civil war ideology, to talk of reconciliation, and to demand that workers and students be allowed to associate freely.

During the war republicans had been responsible for the deaths of about seven thousand people belonging to the church, including monks and nuns. Some two thousand churches were at least partially destroyed. There were horrifying stories of priests being thrown to fighting bulls and, when they had been gored to death, having their ears cut off and awarded to the bulls. The mother of a Jesuit was killed by having a crucifix forced down her throat, and the Bishop of Jaen was killed before a crowd of two thousand people near Madrid. During one priest's trial outside a church, anarchist militiamen got drunk on communion wine, while one used the chalice as a shaving-bowl.

Whether part of Black Spain or the Black Legend, the barbarity of the first few months, in particular, of the Spanish civil war was appalling even by the savage standards of other civil wars. Apart from the war between anarchists and the Church, there were wars between landowners and peasants, between industrialists and workers and between regionalists and military centralists.

Localised civil wars, small armed risings against the government and acts of terrorism had been the rule rather than the exception ever since the Peninsular War. Periods of comparative peace occurred only when violence curbed by dictators had to confine itself to the assassination of leading statesmen. The general civil war which broke out in July 1936 seemed no more than the culmination of more than a hundred years spent preparing for this conflagration; and the violence that was unleashed proved irresistible.

It was suggested at the time, by Professor L. W. Lyde, that countries behave differently according to their geographical situation. Historically, those in latitudes north of 50°N have indulged in what he terms callous cruelty; those south of 45°N in vindictive cruelty. (Interestingly, the 45°N line of latitude passes through Croatia, northern Bosnia and Belgrade.) Where, as in Spain, there had been·no proper penal code or system of legal redress and protection for the poor, the only effective weapon was likely to be private revenge, by vindictive cruelty.

During the civil war the weapon was used to most ruthless effect. Estimates of the number of those, on both sides, who were executed or massacred vary wildly. By the beginning of October 1936 an English correspondent for *The Spectator* was putting the figure at more than one hundred and fifty thousand. Hugh Thomas, in his incomparable history of the Spanish civil war, reckons the total figure for murders or executions behind the lines during the war to have been about one hundred and thirty thousand (seventy-five thousand by nationalists, fifty-five thousand by republicans). What is indisputable is that the vast majority occurred during 1936, when such deaths far outnumbered those killed in action. Some sources have suggested that the rebels executed well over one hundred thousand in Andalusia alone. The Republic held mass executions of fascist suspects dragged from city prisons, including the massacre, carried out by communists in November 1936 at Paracuellos, of up to eight thousand captives taken from jails in Madrid. Both sides also indulged in what were known as *paseos* (walks).

Those who were to be 'taken for a walk' were usually first taken from their homes in motor lorries by a small group of executioners, either at dawn or at dusk. The French writer, Georges Bernanos, who was in Majorca in 1936, was at first sympathetic to the nationalist cause, but changed his mind after hearing of the summary executions which were often carried out with the complicity of the local clergy. He described, in *Les Grands Cimetières sous la Lune*, how Majorcan left-wing sympathisers would be taken for their *paseo*:

> They seized them each evening in remote villages, at the hour of their return from the fields. They departed on their last journey with their shirts still wet, their arms still flushed, from the work of their day – leaving a dinner untouched on the table and a wife who hurries, breathless, to the foot of the garden, with some clothes she has packed. 'Adios.'
>
> 'No need to wake the children; you take me to prison, do you not, *senor*?'
>
> '*Perfectamente*,' replies the executioner, who is sometimes a boy in his teens.

Bernanos also recalls seeing two heaps of corpses – divided according to those who had or had not received absolution – which were doused with petrol and set alight.

On the sixtieth anniversary of the start of the civil war, it is likely that quite a number of these executioners are still alive. I was told of one, Antonio Carrasco, who had supposedly killed eighty-five republicans during the war, in an Andalusian village in the Sierra Morena, and was still living there in the 1980s. A taxi-driver in Seville said that Carrasco had been responsible for the deaths of three members of his family. He felt bitterness and anger, but he was not vengeful. After the bloodbath of the civil war, and the wanton killing within small neighbourhoods, it seemed that revenge had exhausted itself. Carrasco was, of course, shunned by those whose relatives he had killed; but there was no retribution. He stayed on in his village and died in his bed in 1991.

The civil war may be a subject not much discussed these days – according to a 1983 poll, seventy-three per cent of Spaniards considered the war to be a shameful period of their history which was best forgotten – but its impact is still significant. Nearly everyone will have a relative who suffered in the war, even if, as the same poll showed, up to a third of the respondents did not know which side had been supported by Hitler and which by Stalin. True (according to estimated figures), fewer than three per cent (about nine hundred thousand) of the male Spanish population in 1995 could have fought in the civil war. However, there were nearly two and a half million women still living who would have been over eleven years old at the beginning of the war. About twenty-five per cent of the total population would have had a relative who was killed in the war, and probably two thirds a relative who had fought.

To the foreigner, the legacies of the civil war are to be found in a few buildings, and in the experiences of the survivors. The Basilica of the Valley of the Fallen (Valle de los Caidos) is set in a rocky hillside of the Sierra de Guadarrama, north-west of Madrid, where Robert Jordan and his guerrilla fighters were operating in Hemingway's *For Whom the Bell Tolls*. It is a vast and, many would say, grotesque monument to those who died for the 'crusade'. It was constructed, to Franco's basic design, over two decades, employing twenty thousand men, many of them republican prisoners. By the time it was completed in 1959, Franco was comparing its symbolic significance to El Escorial, Philip II's austere palace nearby. The two buildings may conveniently be visited on a day's outing from Madrid (or on the way to Avila and Segovia), but the Valle de los Caidos is memorable not so much for its eight-hundred-and-fifty-foot-long basilica and its five-hundred-foot-high cross on top of the rockface as for the sweated labour which was required to build this egregious memorial. Both Franco and José Antonio Primo de Rivera, founder of the Falange, are buried at the far end of the cathedral cavern, directly beneath the cross on the hill. (They both died on the same date, 20 November, though thirty-nine years apart.) Above their tombs a mosaic dome is embellished with the black flag of fascism, and images of warriors who are variously attired in helmets and battledress, robes and loin cloths.

Much more impressive as a nationalist memorial of the civil war are the remains of the town of Belchite in Aragon, which fell to the republicans, after a long and unequal struggle, in September 1937. At the end of the war Franco decreed that it should be left in ruins as an example of nationalist courage and endurance. Today a few identifiable buildings are still to be seen amid the rubble of the derelict town. It is an affecting testament to the futility of war.

The modern Belchite was built in the 1940s, away from the old town. Approaching from the east, a flat and featureless arable plain gives way to a valley of fruit and olive trees. A signpost indicates that Belchite is one and a half kilometres further on; but there, unsigned and standing above the cross-roads, is the old Belchite of the civil war. The church of San Rafael still dominates what remains of the town, though its spire has gaping holes where the mortar shells struck. When I went there first, on the fortieth anniversary of the battle in 1977, some crumbled houses could be identified by their blue ceramic numbers framed on the walls. The name of a bar – *El Transeunte* (The Passer-by), *Vinos y Licores* – was still legible above a doorway bitten with bullet holes. It was a dead and eerie place: wild flowers were growing in the shell of the church, a group of local children were playing hide-and-seek in the rubble, but there were no other visitors.

Old Belchite did, however, have one resident when I was there. A woman, together with her child, were occupying a makeshift shelter by the arch which gave on to what must have been the town square. She was singing – it sounded appropriately like a lament – while hanging her washing above a rusted tap which carried a notice warning of contaminated water. A more recent visitor to Belchite, in

1995, told me the church spire was still standing, but she had been unable to find *El Transeunte* – the stones on which its name was painted had probably been looted – though she did come across some farm implements in the rubble. On the edge of the old town a gypsy encampment of low, one-storey houses has been built, but her dominant impression was of a chilling atmosphere of stillness about the place. As she left, however, a coach-load of Japanese turned up.

A plaque on a wall of old Belchite refers to the battle as 'one of the most glorious episodes of the crusade'. It was in the last week of August 1937 that the republicans began an attack in Aragon from the east, on a line from north of Huesca to Teruel, with the objective of encircling Saragossa. Franco's attention at the time was directed to the north, where on 26 August the city of Santander fell to the nationalists, who then struck west along the coast and into Asturias. 'They did not abandon their offensive in the north in order to save a small town in the centre,' as Hugh Thomas put it. In effect Belchite and the other small towns on either side of the river Ebro were left to fend for themselves.

In 1937 Belchite was a town of fewer than four thousand people. The republican forces were numerically far superior, and included the five principal International Brigades (it was the first time they had fought together in a combined operation). But the mainly Carlist inhabitants of Belchite withstood the siege for two weeks, in appalling heat and for much of the time without their water supply. The nationalist General Yagüe said of them, 'They are Spanish, therefore they are brave.' But their bravery and resilience astonished the republican attackers, who included several senior Russian officers. Franco did eventually divert some of his forces from the north, and in particular sent air support to Aragon, but it was too late for Belchite, which fell at last on 6 September. Six months later it was easily recaptured by the nationalists; today it is a ghost town, the only surviving relic of the devastation of the civil war. The new town of Belchite was built, as recorded by an inscription in the middle of the modern square and facing the church, in memory of the old town and its 'unequalled heroism' – '*heroismo sin par*'.

Many British volunteers fought at Belchite, with the International Brigades, as they had previously taken part in the battles of Guadalajara,

Jarama and Brunete, and would later fight at Teruel and the Ebro. Laurie Lee described his experience of the Teruel battle, which lasted for most of that terrible winter of 1937–8 (one of the coldest ever recorded in Spain), in *A Moment of War*.

Our machine-gun blew up, and we pulled back down the gully, scrambling and falling over the ice. First I remember a running close-up of the enemy – small, panting little men, red-faced boys, frantically spitting Moors . . . I headed for the old barn where I had spent my first night. I lay in a state of sick paralysis. I had killed a man, and remembered his shocked, angry eyes. There was nothing I could say to him now. Tanks rattled by and cries receded. I began to have hallucinations and breaks in the brain.

When I asked Laurie Lee, in 1995, if he would talk to me about Teruel, he said the memories were too painful. It was only after his death in 1997 that I learnt from Bill Alexander, who commanded the British battalion of the 15th International Brigade at Teruel, that most of Lee's book (the third volume of his autobiographical trilogy) was pure fantasy. He never got beyond Barcelona, Alexander said, never joined the International Brigade and never went near a war zone.

His family disputed this, of course, when I questioned Lee's account in *The Spectator*, but the evidence is against him. Having crossed the Pyrenees in December 1937 and been imprisoned, he met Bill Rust, who represented the British Communist party and undertook to help Lee to join the Brigade. But he failed his medical examination due to epilepsy, and after a while was sent back to England.

Some of the dates and facts, as recorded in *A Moment of War*, just do not make sense. The likelihood is that he was so disappointed not to have fought in the Republican cause that he pretended he had. After more than 50 years (the book was published in 1991) he may even have convinced himself, through the 'hallucinations and breaks in the brain', that he was at Teruel.

One who did see action, and was wounded, at the Battle of the Ebro in the summer of 1938 was Jack Jones, the former general secretary of the Transport and General Workers' Union. He was twenty-five at the time, and had been appointed commissar of the Major Attlee company of the British battalion of the 15th International Brigade. A republican force numbering about eighty thousand began crossing the Ebro in small boats during the night of 24–25 July. In an interview in 1995, Jack Jones told me he remembered being bombed and strafed from the air as he made the river crossing just after dawn.

'Fortunately their bombing was inaccurate, and we continued to advance alongside some Germans [mostly German Jewish volunteers with the Brigades]. The enemy that we encountered consisted mainly of Italians and Moors. We were badly armed and badly clothed, but morale was good for the first few days.'

On 1 August, during an attack on a hill christened by the British 'The Pimple', which overlooked the town of Gandesa, Jones was wounded by a bullet through the right shoulder. 'I had been given a black leather jacket before going to Spain,' he recalled. 'Foolishly I insisted on wearing the bloody thing, which made me rather more visible than others.'

Casualties were heavy; among those killed on that hill were David Haden Guest, well-known communist, and a great friend of Jones's, Lewis Clive. They were both Labour councillors – Clive for South Kensington, Jones for Liverpool, where he worked as an engineer in the docks. It was an unusual friendship forged by war. Clive, descended from Clive of India, had been an Oxford rowing blue and a Guards officer. Jones had stressed to me that the British complement of the International Brigade was essentially, like him, working class and trade unionist. Disproportionate publicity had been given to the few intellectuals and university graduates.

Of the two thousand one hundred British volunteers who went to fight for the Spanish republic, five hundred and twenty-six were killed and between eighty and ninety were still living in 1995. At the end of that year, following an all-party resolution of the Spanish Parliament, they and all other International Brigaders were granted Spanish citizenship. On the sixtieth anniversary of the outbreak of war, commemorations were to be held at the impressive number of memorials to the International Brigade which are to be found in several of our major cities – London, Manchester, Liverpool,

Birmingham, Glasgow, Nottingham. The horseshoe-shaped sculpture on the South Bank, next to the former County Hall, depicting four figures with raised arms and one slumped forward, was unveiled by Michael Foot in 1985. The plinth bears two inscriptions: 'They went because their open eyes could see no other way', and a tribute to those who went 'to fight side by side with the Spanish people in their heroic struggle against fascism . . . Their example inspired the world.'

Jack Jones didn't go to Spain until 1938, but he had been backing the republican cause from the beginning. 'I was a very active trade unionist who was worried about the situation in Germany and in Italy. In the Liverpool docks I was in touch with Spanish seamen; I knew what was happening in Spain and I was anxious to support what seemed to me an important democratic programme – which later became largely the programme of the Labour party.'

After the Jarama battle in 1937, when many of Jones's friends were killed and he was asked to visit their families, he was determined to go to Spain himself and fight. He got there by one of the recognised routes, by train to Perpignan, then over the Pyrenees on foot, in winter and at the mountainous eastern end. He was in a group of twelve, guided over the passes by a Frenchman. 'Some of them said afterwards that was the toughest bit of the war,' Jones remembered. The Spanish winter of 1937–8 was one of the worst ever recorded.

But Jones had good boots – he had been in the Territorial Army – which later were to serve him well at the front. Having reached Figueras in Catalonia, he was sent on to Albacete, where the International Brigades had their training headquarters, under the command of the notorious French communist leader, André Marty. The International Brigades were organised by the Comintern, but probably no more than two-thirds of the volunteers were communists. Jones was commissar, or political officer, of a company, a job he described as being more concerned with the welfare of his comrades. I asked whether he was aware of Soviet influence on the war. The prime minister, Largo Caballero, was in effect removed from office by the communists in 1937; and Jones agreed that 'at that time, the communists were taking over far too much. They wanted all power to central command, to win the war before starting the revolution;

whereas parties like the anarchists and the POUM wanted revolution first – land to the peasants – with which I had some sympathy.'

'But no, I didn't see a lot of Russians, only the occasional "observer". And I had no political liaison with Russians, or with any Spanish politicians: I was just a young brigader. We were given Russian rifles, some of which came to us via Mexico, so we called them Mexicanskis.'

Though a member of a unit which was originally an agency of the Comintern, it is highly unlikely that Jones ever thought of himself as fighting for communism. Rather as Orwell put it in *Homage to Catalonia*, he was fighting against fascism and for common decency.

By the time Jack Jones was wounded, the Brigade's advance had been halted and, though the Ebro battle dragged on into November, with the total number of dead exceeding twenty thousand, this was to be the last republican offensive of the war. (It was during the Ebro battle that Jones's divisional commander, the rough, tough communist colonel, Enrique Lister, was reported to have said to his officers, 'If anyone loses an inch of ground he must retake it at the head of his men or be executed.') Commissar Jones was taken to hospital near Barcelona, invalided out and sent home shortly before the International Brigades were withdrawn from Spain at the end of 1938.

Among other memories, Jones told me that the Germans and Jugoslavs were probably the best fighters, but that the republicans were almost always at a disadvantage because they lacked heavy weapons and air power. Perhaps his keenest recollection was of the lack of food, both at the front and elsewhere.

'We were given that dried cod, *bacalao*, and there were usually some *garbanzos* (chick-peas) for a stew. And occasionally we would find a goat. We couldn't drink the water, so there was a distribution of very crude red wine.

'When I got to Barcelona in the autumn, food was terribly short. In the factories men were literally dropping at their machines from hunger and exhaustion, and in the streets children would come up to you, begging for "*un poco pan*".'

When he returned to England Jones started an appeal in Liverpool for a Spanish food ship. He succeeded in raising some £6,000, by no means all of it from socialist supporters; and the ship reached Barcelona just in time, before the city fell to the nationalists at the end of January 1939.

Food supplies on the other side of the lines, however, were rather better. They may not have been very different at the front; but life in much of nationalist-held Spain seemed largely unaffected by the war, even when battles were being fought not many miles away. In her diary published in 1995,* Priscilla ('Pip') Scott-Ellis, who was nursing behind nationalist lines during the Battle of the Ebro, recounted her visit to the annual *feria* in Saragossa, some forty miles up river from her field hospital. No civil war would stop it taking place, as always, in the second week of October. There were bullfights every day, and plenty of good food: Pip was given ham, sardines, fried eggs and apples for lunch, before going to the hairdresser and then on to the fair to watch a game of pelota. Staying one weekend near Saragossa with cousins of ex-King Alfonso XIII, she referred to 'a huge breakfast' and 'a jolly good tea of toast and lobster paste'. At the end of the war, when she got to Madrid, which had held out against the nationalists for nearly three years, Pip found many people close to starvation. One middle-aged couple in the suburb of Vallecas 'were covered with ulcers and blisters, pouring blood, pus and water, tied up in dirty rags. For two months they have lived on orange peel and a few onions they found fermenting in a manure heap.'

Pip Scott-Ellis was one of about two hundred women from English-speaking countries who served in some capacity (usually nursing) in the war; but there was only one other, Gabriel Herbert, working with Franco's medical services. A very small number of Englishmen also fought for the nationalists in the civil war; one of them, Peter Kemp, met Pip in Saragossa while he was serving with the Foreign Legion. Kemp was a remarkable man: he had no love for Franco or for fascism, but went to Spain – adapting Orwell's reasons for going to war – to fight against communism and for common decency. On more than one occasion he was involved in action against his fellow-countrymen in the International Brigades, one of whom told Kemp

---

* *The Chances of Death: A Diary of the Spanish Civil War*, Priscilla Scott-Ellis (Michael Russell).

after the war that, had he been captured, he would have been shot.

George Orwell may have been fighting against fascism but, having joined the anti-Stalinist POUM militia (Partido Obrero de Unificacion Marxista), instead of the International Brigades, he ended up fighting against communism as well. For four extraordinary days in Barcelona in May 1937, anarchist militants and the POUM were involved in what Raymond Carr describes as 'obscure, complex street and roof fighting' against the communist-dominated Catalan Socialist party. Orwell was sitting on a roof of the Poliorama cinema above the Ramblas, reading Penguin paperbacks, according to his account in *Homage to Catalonia*. The only shot he fired in Barcelona was at an unexploded bomb, which he missed.

In this outstanding book – certainly the best piece of reporting he ever produced – Orwell has some marvellous passages describing the fighting on the Aragon front, of which he saw very little. He once refrained from shooting at a fascist because the man was half-dressed and holding up his trousers. The bombs with which the militia were issued were said to be 'impartial', because they were likely to kill both the man they were thrown at and the man who threw them. 'In trench warfare,' he wrote, 'five things are important: firewood, food, tobacco, candles, and the enemy. In winter on the Saragossa front they were important in that order, with the enemy a bad last.' Not long after the Barcelona May days Orwell was wounded near Huesca and, having got his discharge from the militia, he was lucky to escape from Spain. By that time the POUM had been declared illegal and branded as a fascist agency, not only by the Spanish republican press but by the *Daily Worker* as well. Many of his comrades were imprisoned without trial and shot. Orwell was to say that, as an Englishman, he could never quite believe he would be arrested, as he had done nothing wrong. But he had come face to face with the Totalitarian Lie, with Newspeak. Thereafter the course of his life was set: *Nineteen Eighty-Four* began in 1937, in Barcelona.

That year, as he depicts it in *Homage to Catalonia*, was the watershed of Orwell's life. It was the fulfilment of the years he had spent searching for the proletarian dream – in Barcelona in 1936 the shops and cafés had been collectivised, tipping was forbidden, anyone wearing a tie risked arrest as a bourgeois – and it was the prelude to the disillusion which, having opened his eyes to the methods of totalitarian government, was to lead him to *Animal Farm* and *Nineteen Eighty-Four*. He later wrote: 'Every line of serious work that I have written since 1936 has been written, directly or indirectly, against totalitarianism and for democratic socialism as I understand it.'

Disillusion also occurred among others who saw Soviet communist methods at work. Emma Goldman, an anarchist and feminist who was in her late sixties during the war, wrote of Stalin's 'henchmen who were openly plotting and conniving against the Spanish revolution . . . leaving death and ruin behind them'. Many International Brigaders, while aware that they belonged to an organisation founded by the Comintern, did not appreciate the extent of communist influence and propaganda during the war. There was one small but telling example in a poem written by Alec McDade after the Jarama battle in 1937. It was adopted as the Song of the International Brigades, but not before it had gone through the communist editing process. The first verse began:

> There's a valley in Spain called Jarama,
> It's a place that we all know so well,

And went on, in the official version:

> It is there that we gave of our manhood
> And most of our brave comrades fell.

What McDade in fact wrote was:

> For 'tis there that we wasted our manhood
> And most of our old age as well.

The propaganda continued in the following verses, turning the truth of McDade's words, and the poem was still attributed to him years later (he was killed at the Battle of Brunete in July 1937).

When the International Brigades were withdrawn from Spain at the end of 1938 – by that time the majority of their number were Spanish, and Stalin was contemplating a pact with Hitler – the famous communist leader, Dolores Ibarruri, La Pasionaria (see pages 76–9), gave them a good propagandist send-off in Barcelona. Though many brigaders had had enough of communism, they still looked upon La Pasionaria as symbolising the struggle of the Spanish people against oppression and injustice. Whatever view one takes of the war, she gave a speech which it is still moving to read today (I only wish I could have heard it). She first addressed the women of Spain:

> When the years pass by and the wounds of war are staunched . . . then speak to your children. Tell them of the International Brigades. Tell them how, coming over sea and mountains, crossing frontiers bristling with bayonets and watched by ravening dogs wanting to tear at their flesh, these men reached our country as crusaders for freedom. They gave up everything, their loves, their country, home and fortune – fathers, mothers, brothers, sisters, children – and they came and told us: 'We are here. Your cause, Spain's cause, is ours. It is the cause of all advanced and progressive mankind.' Today they are going away. Many of them, thousands of them, are staying here with the Spanish earth for their shroud, and all Spaniards remember them with the deepest feeling.

Then La Pasionaria spoke directly to the foreigners of the International Brigades:

> You can go proudly. You are history. You are legend. You are the heroic example of democracy's solidarity and universality. We shall not forget you, and when the olive tree of peace puts forth its leaves again, mingled with the laurels of the Spanish republic's victory – come back!

The civil war was, of course, a seminal experience for many British and other foreign volunteers (and a terminal experience for a large number as well). But the freedom for which they were fighting would probably have been largely illusory. It was a social revolution that led to war, but one that became subsumed by outside political forces. If the outcome was a victory for fascism, it was also a defeat for Stalinism. Without foreign intervention, which was crucial to Franco, the republic might well have prevailed; but to what end? The words of the Spanish poetaster, of I know not which century, come irresistibly to mind:

> Free thought I now proclaim to all
> And death to him who does not think as I do.

After almost a century and a half of violence and chaos, and three years of devastating war, Spain was not yet ready, in 1939, to become a modern European democratic state. It had embraced revolution and ended up with a military dictatorship which, as the veteran philosopher, Miguel de Unamuno, put it, had lacked 'reason and right in the struggle'.

Unamuno initially supported the nationalist cause but soon turned against it. At a meeting held in October 1936 at the University of Salamanca, of which he was rector, he famously told his audience, which included Franco's wife and the founder of the Foreign Legion, General Millan Astray:

> This is the temple of the intellect. I am its high priest, and you profane its sacred precincts. You will win because you have more than enough brute force. But you will not win over. For to win over you need to persuade . . . I consider it futile to exhort you to think of Spain.

After the war Franco had no need to argue his case before the Spanish people, or before the rest of the world. The Western democracies withdrew their ambassadors from Madrid and Spain was excluded from the United Nations until 1955. 'Spain lives in truth and sincerity and the rest of the world in perpetual hypocrisy,' was the *generalisimo*'s confident comment on this period, which has been referred to as the Black Night of Francoism but which he thought represented a revival of the Black Legend by a conspiracy of communists.

For all the years of isolation, autarky and repression under Franco, he did nevertheless give to his country a period of peace and stability, and time for recuperation, that was needed before a system of democratic government could be successfully adopted. He also gave Spain back its monarchy, in the hugely successful person of Juan Carlos, who has acknowledged not only his debt to Franco but that the transformation of Spain over which he presided after 1975 could never have been achieved at the end of the civil war.

Two decades after his death, however, Franco has not only receded into history but has become something of a non-person. The obliteration of his memory – streets and squares named after him are now called after the King, statues of him have been taken away – has been almost reminiscent of the totalitarian system which he represented. A young Euro MP for the Popular party, Mercedes de la Merced, encountered a barrage of criticism when she dared, in a public speech in 1994, to give Franco credit for having alleviated the urban housing problem in the 1960s. At the time of the twentieth anniversary of Franco's death, newspaper articles and television documentaries were generally devoted to the years of transition. No more than passing reference was made to the man who, whether he intended it or not, had left his country in a state, and with a constitutional monarch, which made democracy not only feasible but inevitable.

Fewer than five thousand *nostalgicos* attended the 1995 ceremony in Madrid to mark the death of Franco. It was held in the Plaza de San Juan de la Cruz, around a mounted statue of the *caudillo*, the only one that remains in the capital. Blas Piñar, the veteran leader of the neo-fascist Fuerza Nueva, was there, plus many elderly supporters of Franco, a few wearing the dark blue shirt and red beret of the old fascist Falange Española (of which Franco was never a member). They sang their anthem, *Cara al Sol* (Face to the Sun) and gave the fascist salute. The only member of Franco's family to attend was his sixty-nine-year-old daughter, Carmen, Marquesa de Villaverde. Young neo-Nazi skinheads were also present, some from France, Italy, Belgium and Germany. Around the square, street sellers were offering pictures and souvenirs of Franco.

The occasion passed off peacefully, and rather pathetically. One of the organisers, who had expected thirty thousand to attend, tried to fire up the meeting by accusing the King of having betrayed Franco's memory; but he was disowned at once by the leader of the nationalist civil war veterans' association. Even the extreme right, while it retains a chance of playing a more significant political role, is wary of criticising the King.

There was one crumb of comfort for the *nostalgicos* in November 1995: a survey indicated that *franquismo* is looked upon more

benevolently among young Spaniards today. But that may have been because of the increasing contempt with which they regarded the arrogant, autocratic *felipismo* of the man who had been prime minister since 1982. When he came to power as leader of the Socialist Workers' party, the Sevillan lawyer Felipe Gonzalez promised Spain 'a century of honesty'. Thirteen years later, he had lost two deputy prime ministers, five other cabinet ministers, the head of the Guardia Civil, the chief of state security, the governor of the national bank – all because of allegations of corruption made against them. Pedro Ramirez, editor of the newspaper (*El Mundo*) which campaigned to bring down the Gonzalez government, said the scandals for which Gonzalez was responsible made Watergate look like child's play.*

But they posed no threat to Spain's fledgling democracy, which in twenty years had become secure – against political corruption, of which Spain has a long tradition, and political extremism, which can be accommodated within the democratic system. Politically speaking, at least, the blackness of the long Spanish night has yielded to clear, confident day.

* The government of Jose Maria Aznar, a former tax inspector, managed to avoid the taint of corruption for some time after its election in 1996.

FOUR

Soy El Rey

During the Spanish winter of 1937–8 temperatures in the east of the country fell to –20°C. On 5 January, three days before the Aragonese city of Teruel fell to the republican offensive, a baby boy was born in Rome – to Their Royal Highnesses Don Juan de Borbon y Battenberg, Count of Barcelona, and Doña Maria de las Mercedes de Borbon y Orleans. He was the grandson of King Alfonso XIII, who had abdicated the throne of Spain seven years before and, after an interregnum of nearly forty-five years, he would be the next king of Spain. Juan Carlos has played such a remarkable role in the transformation of his country over the past two decades – no one has made a more significant contribution – that it is worth devoting a little space to his life and times.

Juan Carlos did not set foot in Spain until he was almost eleven years old. His childhood was spent in Italy, Portugal and Switzerland (he attended school in Fribourg), with his exiled family and friends such as Gil Robles, the right-wing pre-civil war republican who opposed Franco after 1939, and the Vizcondesa de Rocamora, whose grandfather had been responsible for restoring Juan Carlos's great-grandfather, Alfonso XII, to the throne in 1875. In 1947 Franco 'restored' the monarchy by passing a Law of Succession which defined Spain as a kingdom; but he did not appoint a successor to the throne. Don Juan had effectively disqualified himself by his public declarations and private scheming against Franco, but he did meet Franco on the latter's yacht in the summer of 1948 to agree that the young Juan Carlos should henceforward be educated in Spain.

He arrived in November, by train from Lisbon, on the day that a young monarchist died in a Madrid jail; and he began by attending a small school at Las Jarillas, outside the capital, with seven other pupils, all of them sons of friends of Don Juan. Two years later the school was removed to the Palacio de Miramar in San Sebastian, where he was taught by the headmaster, who was something of a liberal, and a strict Catholic priest, Padre Zulueta. At this period Juan Carlos was living an entirely private life, surrounded only by his tutors and fellow pupils, while holidays were spent with his parents in Portugal.

Things began to change shortly before his seventeenth birthday, when Juan Carlos went to Madrid, to continue his education at the Institute of San Isidro, and for the first time came under military supervision. (One of his military tutors was Alfonso Armada, who was to play a critical role in the attempt to overthrow the government in 1981.) Don Juan wanted his son to go to a foreign university, but Franco persuaded him that a period of military training in Spain would be more appropriate. There followed two years at the military academy at Saragossa, and a year each at the naval academy at El Ferrol and the airforce academy at San Javier. In 1960 Juan Carlos completed his academic education by taking a one-year course in law and economics at Madrid University; and then he started working with his principal tutor and guardian, General Franco. He attended the various ministries, became involved in the workings of government, and lived for a time at the Casita del Arriba next to the Escorial palace outside Madrid. After his marriage in 1962 to Princess Sofia, sister of King Constantine of Greece, he moved to La Zarzuela, a hunting lodge more than a palace, where the royal family still lives today.

It was no doubt embarrassing for Juan Carlos that while he was under Franco's wing his father should continue publicly to criticise the regime and to argue for a constitutional monarchy within a European democracy. Relations were also strained when in 1968, at the christening of the Infante Felipe in Madrid, Don Juan took the opportunity to behave as if he were already the anointed head of state. When Franco finally appointed Juan Carlos his *heredero* (heir) in 1969, it was hardly surprising that Don Juan should refuse to give his blessing. (He did not formally renounce his rights of succession until 1977, when his son had been king for two years.) Franco became so irritated by Don Juan's continued opposition that he banned him from Spain the year before he died.

Franco's last years were known as Juan Carlos's 'silent period': he had no official function, he travelled round the country, looking sullen and, in his own words, 'played the idiot'. He had to be seen to be a *franquista*, because his mentor might otherwise disinherit him – perhaps in favour of his cousin (the son of Don Juan's elder brother Don Jaime) who had married Franco's granddaughter. But Juan Carlos was making important contacts, some from his university days, and he was listening to and soliciting opinions from those of left-wing persuasion. One of his old schoolfriends, José Luis Leal, from his early days in San Sebastian, contacted him from exile in Switzerland, where he was working for the Frente Liberacion Popular. Juan Carlos would often speak to the correspondent of *Le Monde*, sometimes telephoning him from a public call box, and ironically he made contact with Spanish communist elements in Paris through Franco's nephew, Nicolas. He got in touch with the exiled secretary-general of the Communist party, Santiago Carrillo, through President Ceausescu of Romania.

But none of this was known to more than a few people. Juan Carlos was generally thought of as Franco's puppet, who would make few changes after the *generalisimo*'s death. Some, indeed, referred to the new king as Juan *El Breve* – because his reign was not expected to last long. But in his first speech as king, Juan Carlos alluded subtly to the need for change. While paying tribute to Franco's memory, which 'will constitute for me an example of conduct and loyalty', he made a point of calling himself 'King of all the Spanish people'. Juan Carlos was formally committed to the constitution established by Franco, but the old *caudillo* used to say that things would be very different after he was gone; and on his deathbed he said to Juan Carlos: 'All I ask of you, Highness, is to preserve the unity of Spain.'

However, the King's way of going about this would not have been to Franco's liking. In the same inaugural speech Juan Carlos stated that 'a free and modern society requires the participation of all in the decision-making process'. Under the Franco regime Spain had been neither free nor modern but, as Juan Carlos had come to realise in the previous few years, *franquismo* not only should not, but could not, survive Franco. By the 1970s social and economic changes were such that political change was bound to follow. The final Franco years were reminiscent rather of a colonial power that had brought Spain to the point where it was ripe for independence. And I like to think that the wily old dictator would not have felt entirely betrayed by his protégé. Obsessed as he was to the end by the threat of communism, regionalism, anti-clericism and 'the Judaeo-Masonic conspiracy', he would surely have acknowledged that the old order must soon pass away; democratic government could not be resisted for much longer. The speed and extent of the transformation would no doubt have shocked him; but one can credit Franco with having correctly judged that the man he had trained to resume the throne represented the best hope of holding the balance between the authoritarian and liberal instincts of his people.

One of Juan Carlos's principal concerns after Franco died, as he said later, was 'not to make the victors of the civil war into the vanquished of the democracy'. The armed forces needed reassurance that they would not be emasculated by communist influence and other 'threats to national unity', and they looked to the king as their commander-in-chief. In that first speech to the Cortes, he said: 'As the first soldier of the nation, I will ensure that the armed forces of Spain, which are an example of patriotism and discipline, will enjoy the efficiency and strength which our people require.' It was perhaps the first public statement which showed to such effect the King's undoubted talent for equivocation, which he had inherited not only from his former tutor Franco but also from his Bourbon ancestors.

While the King was engaged in keeping the army on side, and at the same time curbing its political pretensions, he moved swiftly to establish a system of parliamentary democracy, revealing a hitherto unsuspected talent for *realpolitik*. His appointee as prime minister, Adolfo Suarez, had been a minister under Franco and was therefore acceptable to the old guard; but he was also a committed democrat. The transformation, by the men and through the institutions of the old regime, was brilliantly achieved, deterring both Right and Left from attempting to sabotage the process. It worked so well that by the middle of 1977, a mere eighteen months after Franco's death, Suarez was able to win power for his coalition of parties (Union de Centro

Democratico) in the first general election to be held in Spain for more than forty years. The parties of the Right and the Communists each received less than ten per cent of the vote. Spain's new constitutional monarch could now afford to take more of a back seat.

The crisis came four years later. The military could not forgive Suarez for having legalised the Communist party; he made matters worse, in their eyes, when he received the head of the Palestine Liberation Organisation, Yasser Arafat (he was the first head of government to do so) and embraced him in public. Suarez was suspected of being half-hearted in trying to defeat Basque terrorism, and by some army officers even of being sympathetic towards the terrorist organisation ETA. Dissatisfaction among the military hierarchy was growing ominously, and there seems little doubt that the King, fearing where this might lead, put pressure on his prime minister to resign. At all events that is what Suarez did, at the end of January 1981, saying that he was taking this action to prevent 'the democratic system we have all desired from becoming no more than a parenthesis in the history of Spain'. But it was too late to put a stop to the plans which were being laid by the captain-general of Valencia and the Machiavellian figure who had been a member of Juan Carlos's household for almost twenty years.

Jaime Milans del Bosch had commanded the Brunete armoured division outside Madrid before he went to Valencia. He had an impressive military family background, with an uncle who had been head of Alfonso XII's military household. He had been with General Moscardo in 1936, as one of the defenders of the besieged Alcázar in Toledo; and he had fought and been wounded in 1942 on the Russian front, serving with the Blue Division. After the 1977 elections Milans wanted to be army chief of staff, and bore Suarez a grudge for having been reponsible for banishing him to the Valencia region. Milans made no secret of his contempt for the changes taking place in Spain, he was a popular figure among his subordinates, and he boasted on more than one occasion that he would bring his tanks on to the streets before he retired. He remained, however, a convinced monarchist, loyal to the King while also fiercely loyal to the memory of Franco.

The Spanish armed forces, in 1981, were still rooted in the past – not just the dictatorships of General Franco, and before him General Primo de Rivera, but in the militarism of the nineteenth century. Military life was ordered in a closed, almost incestuous, society: the army had its own hospitals, clubs and lodging houses; officers were likely to marry officers' daughters; and of those passing through the Saragossa military academy in 1980, sixty-five per cent were the sons of army officers. There was a higher proportion of generals in Spain (1,328 in total, one per four hundred men) than anywhere else in Europe. Most of them were over sixty-three in 1981, and would therefore have fought in the civil war; the transformation of Spain in the late 1970s did not impinge on their lives, except as a threat to the internal security of the country, the defence of which they still considered to be the military's principal role. A newspaper editor at this time commented that while he knew the opinions of each of the leading politicians, he had no idea what high-ranking officers in the armed forces were thinking.

Alfonso Armada was a major in 1954 when he was attached to Juan Carlos as one of his military tutors. He came from an aristocratic background, the son of the Marques de Santa Cruz de Rivadable, and was a godson of King Alfonso XIII. More importantly, he acted as adviser to Juan Carlos on Franco's behalf, vetting the prince's appointments and serving as the *generalisimo*'s watchdog. Armada stayed with Juan Carlos at La Zarzuela until after Franco's death, when he began to manoeuvre himself into a still stronger position. He secured the resignation of the King's private secretary and then started playing politics, sending letters stamped with the royal coat of arms in support of the right-wing Popular Alliance party. General Armada was sent off to Catalonia, to command a mountain division in Lerida, but by the beginning of 1981 he had got himself appointed deputy chief of staff.

So labyrinthine was the plot which led to the attempted coup on 23 February 1981 that it may be simpler not to try too hard to disentangle its various strands. The almost burlesque figure of Lieutenant-Colonel Antonio Tejero, of the Guardia Civil, who invaded the Cortes and held the members of Parliament at gunpoint for several hours, had entered the story more than two years earlier. With other officers, he conceived a plan, at a meeting in the Café Galaxia in Madrid, to seize the Moncloa Palace, the official residence of the prime minister. The plot was discovered and, almost unbelievably, Tejero was given no more than a seven-month prison sentence. No sooner was he out than he was conspiring again to disrupt the democratic process by violent means. This time he met General Milans del Bosch, and the plan was formed to hijack Parliament. The crucial intervention of Armada then convinced Milans they would have the tacit approval of the King, in the wake of Suarez's resignation, to the appointment of a military government of 'national salvation'.

Armada, however, was deceiving Milans on at least two counts: he no longer had the ear of the King, and he intended that, once Parliament had been taken over, he would distance himself from the military coup and step forward as the saviour of the monarchy and of democracy. Fifteen years on, the scenario may seem absurd, but there is no doubt that, in those fevered days in early 1981, democracy was wavering and all that King Juan Carlos had established was desperately at risk.

The attempted *pronunciamiento*, when it came, was not, or should not have been, a total surprise. Rumours were rife of at least two plots – one led by Armada 'in the King's name', and another more violent and obscure in its aims. Then there were the manifestos published in the right-wing daily newspaper, *El Alcázar*, under the pen-name 'Almendros'; they alluded to growing opposition to Suarez in the armed forces and to the need for a 'corrective solution'. The chief of staff of the Brunete armoured division, Colonel San Martin, was said to be one of the authors, and it was assumed that the time for action would be March, when the blossoms on the *almendros* (almond trees) would be at their best. But after Suarez had resigned in the last days of January, the timetable had to be advanced. The final communication from 'Almendros' appeared in *El Alcázar* on 1 February under the heading, 'Decision of the Supreme Command': 'We are at the critical moment . . . the countdown has begun.' On Sunday 22 February, *El Alcázar* carried a front-page photograph of the empty chamber of the Cortes, with a large arrow and the headline, 'Everything is ready for tomorrow's session.' On the same day, it was said that American military bases in Spain were put on alert.

Lieutenant-Colonel Tejero burst into Parliament on the following afternoon at 6.20 pm, while votes were being cast for Suarez's designated successor, Leopoldo Calvo Sotelo. Many of the two hundred civil guards who accompanied him had been recruited only a few minutes earlier and conveyed to the Cortes in buses belonging to Tejero's wife, who had bought them with a loan from a sympathetic businessman. General Milans was able to fulfil his promise by taking his tanks on to the streets of Valencia – he also took over the radio station and arrogated to himself all judicial and police powers – and shortly afterwards he received from Tejero the code words, *sin novedad* (all quiet), which had been used by the rebels at the start of the civil war.

At La Zarzuela the King was about to play squash when the news was brought to him. He put a call through to the chief of army general staff, and Armada came on the line, offering to come out and brief the King in person. A sixth sense, according to Juan Carlos's later account, told him not to let Armada inside La Zarzuela; the general sounded too calm, unsurprised by events in the Cortes, and was offering to contact the captains-general of the various regions on the King's behalf. The King did that job himself, assuring them that the action taken by Milans and Tejero was against the will of the Crown, and assuring himself that they would stay loyal to the person of the King. When Milans said that he had acted only in order to save the monarchy, the King sent him a telex which brought his insurrection to an end. By an extraordinary omission – presumably because the principal conspirators thought they could count on the King's silent support – communications with La Zarzuela were never interrupted. If the telephone lines had been cut, as the King said later, 'and I hadn't been able to get in touch with the captains-general as I did, I don't even like to imagine what might have happened'.

The King was also able to speak to the director-general of Radio Television Española and, although the building was occupied by the armed forces, he ordered the dispatch of a camera crew to La Zarzuela. The statement which he recorded, in the uniform of a captain-general, was broadcast shortly after midnight. The King was seen and heard to be in command, ordering 'all necessary measures to maintain the constitutional order within the legal framework'.

The King's appearance on television confirmed that the coup would go no further. Milans ordered his tanks back to barracks, Armada went to the Cortes to suggest that he might form an interim civilian government, and Tejero threw him out. By dawn on 24 February, Tejero knew he had lost, deserted by both Milans and Armada. But he forced Armada to return to the Cortes to sign the instrument of surrender. Later that day the King received senior members of the government and opposition at La Zarzuela, and the old communist leader, Santiago Carrillo, thanked him for saving their lives. Truly, Spanish democracy had been saved that night by one man.

Yet the part played by the King in this remarkable story has been the subject of much speculation from the Right. Sub-plots were rumoured, while people not only applauded Juan Carlos's courage but commented knowingly that he had also played a typically crafty Bourbon hand. Armada's treachery should have come as no great surprise to Juan Carlos: he had been warned not to trust him many years before, by his father Don Juan, and more recently by his private secretary, José Puig de la Bellacasa, and his prime minister, Adolfo Suarez. In light of the disquiet which some senior officers had privately expressed to the King, the rumours which were current in Madrid towards the end of 1980, and the Almendros articles in *El Alcázar*, it is inconceivable that the King did not suspect that Armada might be involved. When a journalist asked the King, in a private interview in January 1981, whether he knew the identities of Almendros, he gave a Bourbonesque reply: 'I don't know and I haven't been told.' One can be sure, however, that he would have made inquiries. To the question, 'How worried are you by the present unrest within the military?', the King answered that while there were elements within the army that were opposed to everything he was trying to do, the army as a whole would never rise against him. One is tempted to suggest that the King outwitted the *golpistas*, those who were planning to overthrow the democratic government, by doing nothing to stop them until they moved, and then by acting so swiftly and decisively to frustrate the coup that he ensured that no similar attempt would ever be made again.

What seems certain is that both Milans and Armada thought they were acting 'in the King's name'. Milans was organising an army takeover to, as he saw it, save the monarchy; while Armada, in order to pre-empt a military coup, wanted to form a government of 'national salvation', presided over by an unspecified general and loyal to the King as head of state. Those who were drawn to the idea knew Armada to be 'the King's friend' and therefore assumed that the plan had the King's support. At the same time Milans and other senior officers were assured by Armada that the King was privy to their designs.

It is equally clear that, had the King told Milans and Armada that any actions they might be planning to take outside the constitutional framework would be against the King and should be stopped, no coup would have been launched on 23 February. He has since said that he listened to the views of senior officers on the subject of democracy in Spain and told them that if they contemplated anything illegal against the constitutional government, it would be regarded as a direct attack on the Crown. Without wishing to disbelieve this, one is driven to conclude either that officers such as Milans and Armada did not choose to hear the message or that the King did not spell it out clearly enough. It may have been a case of deliberate equivocation; but there is no doubt that the conspirators were led, wittingly or not, to believe they would be acting with the authority of the King.

Critics of the King then say that, when faced with armed invasion of the Cortes and a military takeover in Valencia, he wavered for some hours before deciding not to support the coup. (More than six hours elapsed before the King's appearance on television.) During that time, it was said, the French President, Giscard d'Estaing, offered to send him an aeroplane so that he could leave Spain, and he sought advice from his father, who was sailing off Majorca and told him on no account to go with the army but to stay with his people. It is more likely, however, that the King was resolved, from the time he first heard the news, not to give way to another military dictatorship.

There may have been a Bourbon cunning about Juan Carlos's

action, or rather inaction, before 23 February; but once it happened, he knew that he had to stamp on the insurrection at once or risk going down the same road to exile that his grandfather had taken. Juan Carlos was obsessed with the fact that such a popular monarch, as Alfonso XIII was, should have lost the respect and affection of his people. The reason was simply that in 1923 Alfonso, while remaining king, acquiesced in the overthrow of the constitution by the captain-general of Catalonia, General Primo de Rivera, who established a military dictatorship. I once saw, in the library at Windsor Castle, a book entitled 'Peace, Culture and Progress', a celebration of the reign of Alfonso XIII, published in 1927. It was only four years before the king abdicated his throne and bequeathed to his country a period of political chaos leading to the nightmare of civil war. Juan Carlos was not going to let Milans or Armada become another Primo: that night of 23–4 February was, as a French author described it, Juan Carlos's 'night of consecration' as king. Not only was this military coup at an end; so too was the threat of any more armed risings against the elected government of Spain. The old military guard, experienced in battle both within Spain and elsewhere, has passed away. There are no more veterans of the civil war, no more *africanistas*, on the active list; and democracy is here to stay. At the subsequent trials by military tribunal, Milans and Tejero received long jail terms while Armada got off comparatively lightly with a six-year sentence. He now grows camellias at the family *pazo* (manor house) in Galicia.

Since that critical day, and night, in the history of modern Spain, the King's star has continued in the ascendant. He is respected by Spaniards across the political spectrum who know how crucial he has been to the sea-changes that have taken place in the country over the past two decades. In the 1980s, the old communist civil war general, Enrique Lister, called Juan Carlos 'more liberal than Azaña', president of the Republic during the war. Today the majority of his people see the King as a symbol of steadiness and continuity, as they look ever more contemptuously on the corruption and sleaze in which the government and senior public officials have latterly become embroiled.

The only real criticism of the King seems to come from the Right. There are some retired officers who still consider him 'unpatriotic' for, as they see it, having betrayed Franco; and a few from the old grandee families who take the same view. The latter may also speak disparagingly of the royal family because they have no court, and most of their friends are not from the Spanish aristocracy. There is some surprise, if not resentment, that Juan Carlos hardly ever mentions Franco's name, and it is many years since he attended the annual service at the Valle de los Caidos to commemorate the *caudillo*'s death. However, he will not publicly criticise the man who made him king, nor will he permit anyone to say anything derogatory of Franco in front of him. After all, the King has said, democratic reforms would not have been possible at the end of the civil war; it was Franco who gave to Spain that period of peace which enabled the transition to democracy to be made. The King is also clear that, without Franco's endorsement, he would never have been able to retain the support of the army.

The influence of Don Juan, Count of Barcelona, on his son is something to which Juan Carlos always pays generous tribute. While the relationship inevitably went through a bad patch after Juan Carlos was declared Franco's heir, he recognises that while his father was rebuking Franco for his failure to establish a constitutional monarchy within a European democracy, he was helping to prepare his country for the changes instituted by his son after 1975. Juan Carlos has called his father the most significant Spaniard of the twentieth century and the most unfairly treated. He referred to him, in a film made for television by Selina Scott, as 'my best adviser'.

It was this film, shown in 1993, which drew many people's attention to the more frivolous side of Juan Carlos's character and led to the resignation of one of his longest-serving advisers. The most abiding impression left by the film was of a flirtation between the King and Selina Scott. He very seldom grants interviews to the press, yet here he was pushing his interviewer playfully into the water from his boat.

When she was trying to help him start his motorbike, she touched his arm, giggled, pointed at the choke and invited him to 'pull it out and have another go'. The King enjoys riding his Harley Davidson, though he no longer goes out alone on public roads. Once he helped a student who was pushing his motorbike having run out of petrol. He gave the student a lift to a filling station and took him back with a can of petrol. When the student asked whom he should thank, he stood speechless as the stranger removed his helmet and grinned. '*Soy el Rey*,' he said.

When on holiday in Majorca, the King and his family sometimes dine in a public restaurant. While his informality clearly endears him to his people, his behaviour has on occasion tried the patience of some of his well-wishers. He has been known to leave the country without informing the prime minister of his whereabouts. Once he was embarrassingly absent and out of touch when his signature was required to confirm the appointment of Javier Solana as foreign minister. It was said later that he had gone to Switzerland to attend a course of therapy for burned-out businessmen.

Then there are the King's friends. He has been accused of consorting with an undesirable circle, including a former arms dealer

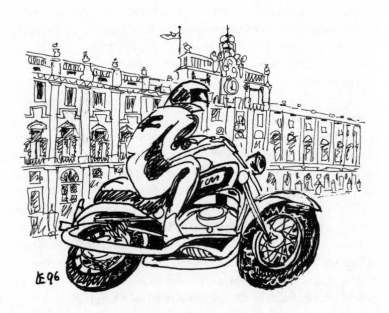

associated with Iraq, a businessman who had dubious dealings with Kuwait, and the owner of a chain of discotheques which were investigated for financial irregularities. The King's long-standing relationship with a Majorcan woman is well-known in Madrid circles. Queen Sofia, who has a strong personality, was said to have tried to get the King to curb his personal lifestyle, enlisting the help of Puig de la Bellacasa, who had returned to the royal household after his stint as ambassador in London. After a few months Puig left La Zarzuela to resume his diplomatic career in Lisbon which, some enjoy pointing out, is in the King's eyes a place of exile. Puig also advised the King to replace some of the old military members of the royal household who were appointed during Franco's time. One of them was General Sabino Fernandez Campo, who resigned, or was relieved of his post, after having criticised the triviality of the Selina Scott film.

After a period of irresponsibility – or should it be called a midlife crisis? – Juan Carlos has appeared more serious. Perhaps the Queen intimated that comparisons might be drawn with his ill-fated grandfather Alfonso XIII, whose playboy reputation would not have been helpful to the survival of the monarchy. But one should not make too much of King Juan Carlos's apparent 'frivolities'. They are very much a part of the Spanish character, and as such quite acceptable to the Spanish people.

The King's abiding concern is that his people should accept not only him as monarch but the institution itself. After all, for the first thirty-seven years of his life, Spain had no king: the restored monarchy is still in its infancy, and the Bourbon dynasty has had a rough ride over the past 150 years. Spaniards recognise, of course, what the King has done for the country since the monarchy was restored. They are overwhelmingly *juancarlista*, but are they *monarquico*? Juan Carlos was expressing this worry not long after the 1981 coup attempt. However, recent widespread corruption in political life, associated principally with the Socialist government in the 1990s, has certainly worked in the monarchy's favour. It may be one of the only institutions to be untouched by scandal. For as long as the corruption in public life continues – and despite a better showing initially from the Aznar government it shows every sign of becoming endemic in Spain – the

71

existence of the monarchy may be thought to provide some check to the perversion of the democratic system and the risk (always present, though dormant, in Spain) of a drift towards anarchy.

There are few who doubt that Felipe, Prince of Asturias and heir to the throne, will succeed his father as king. He is popular, seemingly serious-minded, better educated than his father (he has attended colleges in the United States and Canada), and a better sailor too (he competed in the 1992 Olympics). He is likely to be the first king of Spain to have an uninterrupted reign, and to be born and die in his own country, for about two hundred years.

FIVE

Women and Country Life

There was not much emancipation for women during the Franco years. In rural areas, particularly in the south, it was almost unheard of for a woman to work outside the home until the 1960s; and the Church continued to give its support to the status quo. Women were expected, of course, to work the family plots of land while their husbands were away earning their living, perhaps in the construction or fishing industries. But the gradual liberation of country women did not occur until large-scale migration to the cities began about a decade before Franco's death.

At that time the *permiso marital* still governed relationships between husband and wife, providing for an almost totally one-sided marriage contract that was enshrined in the Spanish Civil Code. The wife could not, without her husband's permission, take a job, buy and sell goods or open a bank account. If she left home for a few days without her husband's approval, she risked being accused of desertion. A woman's adultery was a crime in any circumstances, but a husband could misbehave with impunity, so long as he didn't do it in the matrimonial home or live with his mistress. The easiest, and most acceptable, course for a married man was to use the services of a prostitute, of whom there were around five hundred thousand in 1970, or one in twenty-seven of the adult female population. Many of them were driven 'on the game' by the lack of assistance for single mothers and of job opportunities.

But Spanish women have come a long way in the past few years. The number of working women increased by nearly fifty per cent in the 1980s; the doctrine of equal rights was officially sanctioned in 1988 with a *Plan para la Igualdad de Oportunidades de las Mujeres*. Women represented no more than a quarter of the total working population in 1980. The figure had risen to thirty-six per cent by 1995, but was still below the European Community average, which then stood at forty-two per cent.

In the first two decades of Spain's modern democracy, the mould was broken in several areas of professional life. A female cabinet minister was appointed in the late 1970s, and more recently a woman governor of a men's prison and a chairwoman of a league football club. Female judges are now quite commonly appointed, and the prime minister, Jose Maria Aznar, brought four women into his first cabinet. In 1995, for the first time, there were more female than male entrants to the civil service; several large cities had lady mayors, most of them representing the Popular party; and in Alicante province a town council was controlled by women. Lady matadors are now appearing in the bullring on foot, having been allowed for years only to fight on horseback.

If Spanish women are catching up fast, some traditional family attitudes still remain. A survey, carried out in 1991, of the division of responsibility for domestic work – cleaning the house, preparing breakfast, washing dishes, making beds – showed that the vast majority of men not only thought of it as women's work but were not in favour even of sharing the household chores. One of the objectives of the Equal Opportunities Project is expressed to be 'to encourage fair sharing of domestic and family tasks . . . by promoting social awareness of equal distribution of household duties and its social value'. Older men, in particular, may sniff contemptuously, but it will not be long in coming.

Between north and south there is probably still a wide disparity in attitudes to the place of women in society. In rural churches in Estremadura I have seen men and women sitting separately; and many Andalusian girls are still kept behind closed doors – a legacy, no doubt, of eight centuries of Islam. The more liberated status of women in the north may owe something to the matriarchal society said to exist there in pre-Roman times. In the nineteenth century George Borrow noted, in *The Bible in Spain*: 'The Basque females differ widely in character from the men; they are quick and vivacious, and have in general much more talent.' It certainly appears to be the case that famous Spanish women of the past have come from the north. One

thinks in particular of Maria Pita, who saved Corunna from capture by Drake when she slew the English standard-bearer; and, in this century, of Dolores Ibarruri, known as La Pasionaria. I wonder how long it will be before another woman in Spain enjoys as much fame as was achieved by that extraordinary political figure who died, a month before her ninety-fourth birthday, in 1989.

'That bitch' were the words used by a nationalist veteran from the civil war, when I ventured to express my admiration for the force of La Pasionaria's extraordinary personality. She was certainly one of the moving spirits behind the republican forces in the war, and the most famous Spanish woman of her generation. Although a committed communist from an early age, La Pasionaria ('the Passion Flower') inspired people as much by her undoubted courage, the power of her oratory and her presence – she was very tall and always dressed in black – as by her belief in the Russian Revolution.

In the first months of the war no face or voice on the republican side was better known than hers. The posters in Madrid portrayed Lenin, Stalin and La Pasionaria, rather than the president or any other politician. Not only did she lead the recruiting campaign for the republican army in rousing, often fanatical speeches on the wireless and at mass rallies, but she had a battalion named after her.

The name of La Pasionaria is most often associated with her rallying cry at the beginning of the war, '*No pasaran!*' ('They shall not pass!') – echoing Petain at Verdun. No less memorable were her exhortations to Republican troops to 'die on your feet rather than live on your knees', and her speech of farewell to the International Brigades in Barcelona when they were withdrawn in 1938 (see pages 52–3).

It was remarkable that any woman, in Spain and in time of war, should be as influential and famous, or notorious, as the Communist deputy for Asturias. Inevitably, La Pasionaria's reputation led to stories told on the nationalist side of her cruelty, in particular towards prisoners and nuns. She was described, quite wrongly, as a former nun who had married an unfrocked monk and cut a priest's jugular vein with her teeth.

In fact, in contrast to the ferocity of many of her speeches, there were several instances of La Pasionaria's compassion during the war.

Oddly, as the fount of revolutionary womanhood, she did not support the call for women to take up arms, urging them instead to leave the front and assist the war effort by working in factories or hospitals. She also played a leading role in educating the peasant militiamen. It was said that when a soldier had been taught to read and write he would write two letters – one to his wife and the other to La Pasionaria to tell her that he was not only fighting the fascists, but learning as well.

Throughout the war La Pasionaria held rigidly to the Communist party line, often disagreeing with Largo Caballero's and Negrin's conduct of the war and consistently opposing the anarchists and the POUM. In her autobiography, *El Unico Camino* (published in Britain under the title of *They Shall Not Pass*), she writes disingenuously of the 'unconditional aid' given by Stalin to the Spanish Republic and of the Russian 'volunteers' who supported it. She maintained the position prescribed by Moscow, and at the same time devised a spurious defence of property rights to keep the middle classes in the republican camp. In 1939, at the end of the civil war, she left the 'rats of capitulation' for exile in the Soviet Union, where she was to spend the next thirty-eight years.

Dolores Ibarruri had been born in 1895, the eighth of eleven children, to a mining family in the Basque country. Her upbringing was harsh, and at fifteen she went to work as a seamstress, then as a domestic servant, resentful that women could not work in the mines. Dolores's marriage, at twenty, to a miner, followed by the birth of a daughter, did nothing to alleviate her poverty; she began to lose her previously strong religious convictions and to read Marx and Engels. Her husband was often in prison, and three of her children were to die in infancy.

Shortly after the Russian Revolution, writing in a journal called *The Class Struggle*, Dolores signed her article Pasionaria, and the name stuck. She joined the Basque Communist party in 1920 and was elected to the central committee of the Spanish Communist party (PCE) ten years later.

The declaration of a republic brought little of the 'democratic progress' envisaged by the Communists, and La Pasionaria was jailed several times in Madrid and Bilbao. She paid her first visit to Russia in

1933 for the thirteenth Communist International and described Moscow as 'the most marvellous city in the world'. She was back in prison again in January 1936, shortly before the election of a Popular Front government and her own election as one of seventeen Communist deputies. One of her first acts was to open the doors of Oviedo jail. Most of the prisoners had been held captive since 1934, when General Franco (who was married in Oviedo) was sent to Asturias to put down a revolution led by the coal miners – which he did, using Moorish troops and brutal force.

In Parliament she was scathing in her attacks on 'the forces of reaction'; she was blamed, unfairly, for having instigated the assassination of Calvo Sotelo a few days before the uprising in July. During the civil war La Pasionaria and the Communist ministers were often critical of the government for its irresolution and failure to take advantage of republican military successes. She had a special affinity with the International Brigades and the foreign visitors to the republican zone, who seemed to symbolise for her a world-wide fraternity of revolutionary idealists fighting fascist oppression. And they looked to her, staying on in Madrid after the government moved to Valencia in November 1936, as the figure who more than anyone else gave inspiration to their cause.

The British members of the International Brigades honoured her in 1979 with a memorial in Glasgow. And her fame in the 1930s was such that Picasso dedicated a number of paintings to La Pasionaria, and she was widely believed to have been the inspiration for Pilar in Ernest Hemingway's novel, *For Whom the Bell Tolls*.

During the long years of exile, La Pasionaria travelled to most other Communist countries; by the time she returned home, after Franco's death and the legalisation of the PCE, she had been slavishly following the Moscow party line for the best part of sixty years. Not surprisingly, she found herself out of touch with the new generation of young Eurocommunists, to whom she became something of an embarrassment. She was discouraged from speaking in public.

But, forty years on, she was elected once again to the Cortes as deputy for Asturias, though she was to retire soon afterwards. In spite of her differences with the PCE, she continued to go, almost daily, with her lifelong friend Irene Falcon, to the party's headquarters in Madrid. And on her ninetieth birthday she made her last major public appearance at a rally and was given the Order of the October Revolution.

Me Faltaba Espana (*I Missed Spain*) was the title of her second volume of memoirs, published in 1985; but one wonders what she made of the democratic, westernised Spain that was emerging when she came back. Of La Pasionaria and other old republicans, John Hooper wrote in *The Spaniards*: 'With their intemperate language and their intransigent attitudes [they] seemed to the left-wingers and regional nationalists of the seventies like creatures from another planet.' For La Pasionaria, too, modern Madrid, and cities such as Oviedo, which she first represented in 1936, must have seemed unrecognisable.

Today one might expect Oviedo to be something like Newcastle, a modernised industrial centre, whereas it resembles much more closely a smaller version of Madrid. There are shops selling exotic chocolates, expensive leather goods, jewellery, kangaroo-skin shoes, fur coats; one might almost be in the Calle de Serrano or in Bond Street. Sitting one afternoon in the Parque de San Francisco, I saw young women sauntering by with a self-confident air, shouldering a smart bag and often smoking a cigarette. I heard one laughingly use the word *machista* (sexist) to a man fashionably dressed in tweed jacket and grey flannel trousers.

There would be little chance of any mutual understanding between this *guapa* in modern Oviedo and the old black-clad revolutionary. But the emancipated Spanish women of today, doing business with men and being treated by them on equal terms, would do well to acknowledge the role of La Pasionaria in the evolution of women's rights and aspirations in Spain. They need not share her revolutionary ideals in order to recognise her as a pioneering feminist force.

Nowadays black is regularly worn only by the old women of poorer families. With the adoption of modern European dress by almost all women below the age of fifty, the days of the *abuela* (grandmother) in black, except during times of mourning, are surely numbered. (In Gerald Brenan's Andalusian village, in the 1920s, all married women over the age of twenty-five wore black.) But if dress fashions are changing within the family, attitudes to marriage among rural families remain largely unaltered. A boy and girl may go out together more openly these days, but the *novio* will not be admitted to the living-room of his girlfriend's parents unless and until they are engaged.

To appreciate the enduring significance not only of marriage in a Catholic country but of the wedding ceremony in Spain, you have only to look in the window of one of the bridal shops to be found in every provincial town. The wedding dress may be diamanté, with pale pink roses on the shoulders and a pearl-studded bodice. There will be satin gloves, also studded with pearls, tiaras, thigh ribbons, gold coins, heart-shaped cushions, plastic horseshoe bouquets. Bridesmaids' dresses are provided, also hats, bags and black lace gloves for the bride's mother. In one shop window in Merida I saw a wax model of a page in tail-coat with red cummerbund and matching tie, with an elaborate tie-pin and a crucifix in the buttonhole.

In spite of the diaspora – whether due to married couples moving away or to sons and daughters going to work in the city – village families are often reunited, for weekends, *fiestas* and the annual *matanza* (see page 85). Family ties may be stronger now that the mass migration to the cities, which took place in the 1960s, has come to a halt.

Improved roads have encouraged new building (not all of it hideous) on the outskirts of almost every Spanish village. Some of the houses will belong to 'incomers' and weekenders but, unlike in Britain, the community life of the village has not been lost. This is largely because, however much it is transformed, the village or small town in Spain retains its hub. This is the central *plaza* where people, and especially women, meet and chat – outside the church, or the shops, in the café or while taking an early evening stroll (*paseo*). There is nothing new about this tradition, but these days many of the women will be younger, more colourfully dressed and smoking cigarettes.

* * *

You don't find many large country houses in Spain. Among the aristocracy, the owners of rural estates are usually absentee, visiting their property only infrequently from Madrid or Seville and preferring to stay in a spacious modern bungalow rather than the old farmhouse or olive mill, which will probably be semi-derelict anyway. Equally, in the eighteenth and nineteenth centuries, grandee Spaniards spent little time on their estates: they did not build grand houses, and there was no country house life as we know it in England. In part this was due to lack of water and communications – much of Spain is either dry, or mountainous, or both – also to the likelihood of being threatened, or worse, by marauding bandits.

The *finca* of Pascualete, near Trujillo in Estremadura, has been in the same family for many generations; the house is mainly sixteenth-century, though with origins going back to the Romans. However, until the American-born Condesa de Quintanilla dragged her husband there in the 1940s, no member of the family had set foot on the property for more than a hundred years.* The principal reason for this was the aftermath of the Peninsular War. Many parts of the country were ravaged and laid waste by the French invaders: buildings and bridges were demolished and lawlessness prevailed in much of rural Spain for years afterwards. (Richard Ford testified to this, in his *Handbook for Travellers in Spain.*) At the same time new taxes were levied on large landowners, leading them to abandon their provincial estates and head for the cities. It took the enthusiasm and enterprise of an American woman to persuade the Conde de Quintanilla that his ancestral home could be restored and made habitable, even by the metropolitan standards of comfort to which he was accustomed. The partridge and bustard shooting was, of course, an added incentive.

Sixty miles away, to the north-east, on the Estremadura–Toledo border, I was invited to stay with a ducal family who had been spending Christmas and Epiphany together on their fifteen-thousand-acre estate near Oropesa. They would disperse before the end of January, some to Madrid, others to New York, but the house would be occupied by at least one family member for about three months of the year. It consists of an eighteenth-century farmhouse with several single-storey extensions around a tower and courtyard.

* *The Story of Pascualete*, Aline Quintanilla (John Murray, 1963).

Follow the unmade road, I was told, north towards the Sierra de Gredos for eighteen kilometres, past oak woods, cattle pasture and across dried-up stream beds, and you will reach the house. (It was in fact only ten kilometres from the main road – Spanish grandees of my acquaintance are prone to exaggeration – but still pretty impressive for a private drive.) After three kilometres you have to cross the unguarded Madrid–Lisbon railway line. The Duke used to have his own station on the estate, but the trains don't stop there any more.

After the civil war there was an engine-driver, on one of the Pacific coal trains, who was in the habit of taking his two greyhounds with him on the footplate. The Duke would allow the train to stop on his land so that the engine-driver's dogs could course the hares; and in return the Duke was permitted to fulfil a childhood ambition by driving the train down the line as far as Navalmoral de la Mata.

One bright but chilly Sunday morning, when the Duke was sitting on the terrace, wearing a camel-hair overcoat and green felt hat, I asked him about the civil war. As a twenty-two-year-old monarchist student in 1936, he was staying in Madrid with a member of the British embassy at the outbreak of war. Ignoring the Union Jack that was hanging outside the flat, republican militiamen soon found and arrested the young Marquess (which he then was). He was taken before a *checa* run by anarchists and briefly interrogated. He thought he would be shot. The suspicion became certainty when he was taken down to a windowless basement and pushed against a wall, facing a squad of militiamen who raised their weapons.

'You're going to die now – you and all your class,' said one, as they took aim. The Marquess remembers that his predominant feeling at this moment was anger; he took a few steps forward, shouted an insult and declared his innocence. Suddenly the men lowered their rifles and one of them began to laugh, saying that the death sentence was being postponed. He was kept imprisoned in a school building for several weeks until, one morning in September, a man called Juliá turned up, apparently from the economic section of the British embassy, and the Marquess, together with two companions who had been arrested with him, was allowed to leave.

'The British embassy had interceded with the republican government on our behalf,' the Duke recalled sixty years later, 'because we had been wrongly arrested in a diplomatic flat, which was British property. I imagine that our anarchist captors [members of the Federacion Anarquista Iberica] did not want to fall out with the government over my case, and so they released me.' Having hidden in an embassy building for a few days, the Marquess made his way to Atocha railway station, dressed in overalls and carrying forged identity papers. As he was about to board a train to Alicante, his old Irish nanny, Nellie Cunningham, turned up on the platform, bringing him whisky and cigarettes. 'My darling boy!' he heard her call out. In other circumstances the Marquess might have imagined himself taking part in a scene from an Ealing comedy. He never discovered how his nanny had learnt of his whereabouts, but he knew she was endangering his life at this moment and urged her to leave him.

During the journey to the coast the Marquess was recognised by a republican militiaman but made his escape from the train just before it reached Alicante. There he contacted some Italian naval officers, who took him on board their destroyer in the guise of an Italian deserter, and thence to La Spezia. Two years later he returned to nationalist Spain and fought in the Foreign Legion until the war ended in 1939.

The Duke took a piece of home-cured ham from the table. 'It was the only time during the war that the Reds broke into property under British protection,' he said. 'I was very grateful for what the embassy did for me, though I think one of their staff, called Malcolm, was a Red.'

To the nationalists in those days, the enemy were all Reds, while the republicans would say they were fighting the fascists. The Duke was never a fascist, but he would not be told that perhaps some of the other side were not actually communists.

'Down the road in Oropesa, the Reds committed a terrible atrocity at the beginning of the war,' he told me. 'They herded most of the *petite bourgeoisie* of the town – shopkeepers, professional people, nuns – into the courtyard of what is now the *parador*, and was then occupied by the Guardia Civil. It used to be the palace of the Counts of Oropesa.

'There is a medieval castle opposite and the courtyard is walled on all sides. Into this enclosed area the Reds then let loose some fighting bulls. When Yagüe's Army of Africa got there a day or so later, everyone in the courtyard was dead.'

When I went to the *parador* the following night, the courtyard was empty except for a few cars, and eerily lit by a full moon. From the Capilla de San Bernardo came the rat-a-tat of a stork's bill. For a moment I thought it might be a machine-gun . . . a revenge killing by the nationalists before they swept on to Toledo to raise the siege of the Alcázar.

Storks nesting on church towers are a common enough sight in this part of Spain – some of them now seem to be resident all year round – while a number of species of large birds can be glimpsed on the Duke's estate. A few miles to the west, the national park of Monfragüe is home to Spanish imperial eagles, Bonelli's eagles, black vultures, griffon vultures, cranes, black storks, kites, bustards – not to mention a large variety of mammals, such as lynx and genet, and nine species of snake. It is possibly the best area of Spain for wildlife – even more prolific and varied than the Coto Doñana.

This is *dehesa* country: cork oaks and holm oaks are thinly planted – and harvested for cork and charcoal – while the pasture underneath, and the acorns, are grazed by cattle and pigs. Oats are also grown here for the cattle, but the acorns are judged to be important in giving more flavour to the meat.

One day we toured part of the estate in a wagonette, drawn by two ponies. Near the western perimeter, we crossed a *camino real* – an old drovers' road used for taking cattle and sheep between summer and winter pasture. It runs north-south, the entire length of Spain, from Galicia to Huelva, and parts of it are still used for its original purpose. It remains a public right of way. Dusk was falling as we returned to the house, the ponies zigzagging between the oak trees, scattering lapwings and hoopoes from their path. A party of pigeon-shooters were preparing to take their bag home to Oropesa while, overhead, a skein of greylag geese honked by, heading south to the River Tagus.

Dawn broke soon after eight the next morning, and the rising sun was flickering through tall eucalyptus trees as the farm workers came across the frosted ground to assemble in a shed in the yard. Breakfast was being prepared over an open wood fire. It consisted of small pieces and crumbs of bread (*migas*), soaked in olive oil and garlic and fried briefly in a pan. We took them with spoons from the pan; coffee and red wine were handed round in mugs. It was delicious, but not an everyday breakfast. Today was special because it was the day of the killing of Alvaro's pig.

There is something akin to a 'pig culture' in western Spain. *Matanza* is the word for the ceremonial slaughter of a pig, which takes place every winter, usually in January, though sometimes on the day after Christmas. The Iberian pig is big and black and well fattened, and on many estates, such as this one, it traditionally forms part of a farm-worker's annual wage. In *The Story of Pascualete*, the author relates how the pig is grasped by four men, who tie its hind legs together. The pig-killer, armed with a knife, then approaches the animal from behind, grabs it under the chin, locates the jugular vein and plunges the knife in. A bucket is then placed under the neck to catch the draining blood, the hairs of the pig are carefully singed and shaved, and the skin is scrubbed until it is white. Only then does the butchery begin, with each limb and organ of the animal being delicately removed and washed in deep buckets of water.

I missed the killing of the pig and it was after dark when I got to Alvaro's cottage. His wife and children, and several other helpers, were busy making *chorizo* (spiced sausage) and *morcilla* (blood pudding) in an adjoining shed lit only by candles and a blazing fire. The mixtures were being pressed through mincers and into skins which, when about eighteen inches long and horseshoe-shaped, were strung up on a washing line hanging from the ceiling. One child fell back into a wooden vat half-filled with *morcilla* and flavoured with onion and pumpkin. The man who was working the mincer laughed so much that his cigarette fell out of his mouth. A *bota* (wineskin) was passed round, and we dug our fingers into the sausage mixtures. A woman wearing a shawl held a small child in a rocking-chair by the fire.

It was a scene reminiscent of one of Velazquez's early paintings of tavern scenes (*bodegones*) – except for the two-way radio standing on a ledge above the fireplace. Next door, more women and children, one of them screaming intermittently, were watching television in a simple living-room with round table and gas stove. On the patio legs of ham, and most of the pig's other parts, hung from a line propped up by forked staves. Illuminated only by the coals of a brazier, one pendulous piece looked something like an unusually long pair of studded, pink and white tights. The pig's heart hung from the rope line like a giant ruby on a necklace. Indoors, the extruding of the *chorizo* and *morcilla* continued, and the *bota* was refilled with wine. The camaraderie seemed the more tactile for the fact that outside the temperature was below freezing. On the way home, in the back of an open jeep, we huddled under a blanket and I kept my hands warm against the throat of our host's spaniel. Two hares darted uncertainly across the dirt track. Halfway up the slopes of Mount Almanzor, the highest peak in the Sierra de Gredos, a fire was burning.

Before dinner that evening – which began at 11 pm, late even by Spanish standards – we ate slices of home-grown ham, cured in the cold air of the sierra, and discussed the significance of the pig in Spain's culture. The Duchess made the point that it helps to keep families together: those who have left their rural roots and gone to work in the city will always return to their villages at the time of the *matanza*. Like a wedding or funeral, it is a family occasion. In Madrid El Museo del Jamon – a chain of bars with hams and sausages hung all over the walls and ceilings – provides a picturesque reminder of the importance of the pig in Spanish gastronomy. Suckling pig *a la espalda* (with trotters splayed and its head on) is often to be seen in restaurant windows; and on more than one occasion I have been offered a stew of pig's ears.

Some of these pigs may be crossed with wild boar, and are to be treated with care. At Pascualete, one amateur slaughterer had his hand pierced by a tusk; and in Camilo Jose Cela's famous novel, *The Family of Pascual Duarte*, Pascual's brother, Mario, has his ears chewed off by a pig.

Conversation at dinner turns to the harshness of village life in the old days. Gerald Brenan had once told the Duke that the poor were, in a sense, 'better off' then, because more affluent times had brought a climate of envy and antagonism between families. Where there was poverty, or strife, there was also pride – a quality highly prized by

86

Spaniards. (To say of a man that he is *sin vergüenza* – without shame – is the greatest insult.) The story is told of a beggar who was given alms by a passer-by and then asked to cross the road and get a newspaper for his benefactor. But he refused: 'I am a beggar, sir, not a messenger.' The Duke recalled the pride and dignity with which his fellow nationalist prisoners bore themselves when they were taken away to be executed. The evening ended stirringly with the Duke's son playing a recording of the hymns which his father had sung in the Spanish Foreign Legion.

SIX

Culture in the Afternoon

The man who introduced me to bullfighting, Vane Ivanovic, once wrote that 'cricket in England and the national *fiesta* of bullfighting in Spain are just about the only two civilised pastimes left in Europe'. It was a nicely provocative statement, and he went on to compare the ethos of cricket (as it used to be played) and bullfighting. The result is unimportant – in a bullfight it is pre-ordained – but what does matter is 'how you played the game'. He also wondered if it was mere chance that the national flag of Spain is identical to the colours of the Marylebone Cricket Club.

Note that Ivanovic referred to bullfighting as a pastime. It may be also be called a spectacle, even an art; but it is not a sport. The bull always loses: *matador* means killer, and if he is put out of action by the bull's horns, another matador will do the job (which is the literal translation of *faena*, as the last stage of a fight is called). Bullfight is an inadequate translation of what Spaniards call a *corrida de toros* (running of the bulls), as part of the *fiesta brava* (noble festival). It has to be understood, for those who wish to understand it, in the context of Spanish culture. Reports of *corridas* in the Spanish press appear in the cultural, or arts, sections of the newspapers.

Perhaps it would be better not to write about the bullfight in English. Feelings on the subject can be somewhat extreme. After publishing an article about a matador in *The Spectator* I received a letter, from a reader

in Warwickshire: 'It would make the world a cleaner place if he wound up with a bull's horn up his arse, preferably with the other horn up yours.' The majority of English-speaking people consider bullfighting to be a barbarous practice which has no place in modern society; and it may be thought presumptuous of those of us who are *aficionados* to try and interpret what no Anglo-Saxon can ever fully comprehend. But we can still make a few points and dispel a few myths.

It is certainly true that a lot of rubbish has been written in English about bullfighting. Many have been able to see it only in terms of religious ritual and sexuality. When it fell to me to review, for the *The Times Literary Supplement*, a social history of bullfighting published by the University of Pennsylvania Press, I was riveted to learn about the masculine and feminine roles played by matador and bull. It had simply never occurred to me that the sword symbolised a phallus and the cape the female genitalia.

Hyperbole is never far away, in books on bullfighting, even from the best writers on the subject, such as Ernest Hemingway and Kenneth Tynan. When Antonio Ordoñez was fighting, Hemingway wrote, 'you felt your chest and throat tighten up and your eyes dim seeing something that you thought was dead and done with come to life before you'. Tynan was also moved to write of Ordoñez, when he fought with Litri in Valencia in 1952, that 'Reach [Litri] was confronted with Grasp [Ordoñez], Accident with Design, Romantic with Classic, Sturm und Drang with Age of Gold.'

As a left-wing theatre critic and opponent of capital punishment, Tynan must have seemed, to some, an unlikely supporter of bullfighting. He saw it in dramatic terms: quoting C. M. Bowra on the task of the epic hero, he neatly defined the bullfight as representing 'the pursuit of honour through risk'. Someone else has written of the matador aspiring 'to invent an aesthetically pleasing performance with a somewhat unpredictable animal that is trying to kill him'. There is no doubt that the principal fascination of the spectacle is in watching a man voluntarily put himself so close to death.

Until the eighteenth century, bullfighting was practised only by the aristocracy; they fought the bull from a horse with lances. At least one pope and one king had tried unsuccessfully to ban the *corrida*. It was the peasants in the countryside who were most passionate in their enthusiasm for the bulls; unable to afford horses, they developed the technique of modern bullfighting on foot.

From this period, according to Ortega y Gasset, the history of *la fiesta brava* 'reveals some of the best-kept secrets of Spanish national life over almost three centuries'. As the aristocratic *toreo de rejones* gave way in the eighteenth century to the practice of the peasant class to run the bulls on foot, so the nobility, educated in French attitudes and tastes, failed to sell the ideals of the Enlightenment to the Spanish people. The ruling class began to lose its moral authority, to abdicate social responsibility, and it was left to the people, inspired by their new-found success in taking over the conduct of the bullfight, to provide the real resistance to the French invader Napoleon.

It has been argued that bullfighting is the legacy of obscurantism: bread and bulls kept the people quiet for two centuries, and democracy in the ring delayed its extension into political life. It was thought that bullfights and cruel Catholic dictatorships went hand in hand. There was something about the violence, and the ritual, which could readily be associated with Franco's repressive regime but which would clearly not survive Spain's transition to a liberal, socialist society and its emergence into the modern European world.

It is pleasing to record that such a supposition – wishful thinking, perhaps, on the part of those who would label themselves 'civilised' and 'politically correct' – has proved totally false. All political parties embrace the bullfight as folk art and matadors as men of the people. It is, after all, *la fiesta nacional*, followed alike by Andalusian villagers, because modern bullfighting originated in the south, by Madrid 'yuppies', because it is fashionable, and by intellectuals because it is part of Spanish culture. Government ministers like to be seen at the *plaza de toros* of a Sunday afternoon (bullfighting laws come under the Interior Ministry); the King attends important fights in Madrid, and his mother, the Countess of Barcelona, is a devoted *aficionado*. At the time of his accession Juan Carlos said that his only regret on becoming king was that it would leave him less time to go to the bulls. (His Greek-born wife, Queen Sofia, does not share his enthusiasm.)

In 1994 bullfighting was flourishing under socialism: more corridas were held during the season than ever before, and one man, Jesulin de Ubrique, fought on one hundred and fifty-three occasions, easily breaking the record, set in 1970, of the famous, and meretricious, Beatle bullfighter El Cordobes. To those who might say that there must be a lot more *corridas* staged for the tourists these days, statistics show that the reverse is true. Whereas more than a third of the fights in 1971 were held in Mediterranean rings with a major reliance on the tourist trade, that proportion had fallen to ten per cent by 1994.

Unquestionably, the increased popularity of bullfighting is due to larger Spanish audiences.

And then there is the television coverage. More than three hundred *corridas* were televised in 1994, getting on for twice as many as in the previous year. One June day in San Sebastian, I was able to watch bullfights live on three different channels – and highlights, plus interviews with the principal matadors, later that evening. Animal rights campaigners would not like to have to admit it, but bullfighting today enjoys a much wider popularity in Spain. Because of television, the *corridas*, or rather the individual *toreros*, are discussed in offices and supermarkets. The best-known, Jesulin, who had his twenty-first birthday in 1995, fought six bulls the previous year in Aranjuez in front of an entirely female audience, who threw flowers, underwear and finally themselves into the ring.

The matadors today come from a wider cross-section of society: the image of hungry, penniless boys wandering round Andalusia to fight in village *capeas* and bull-breeders' *tientas*, in the hope of getting noticed, is no longer valid. Some *toreros* have university degrees these days; others come from rich bullfighting families. Feminists should be pleased to learn that in 1994 there were three women matadors, and Eva Armenta became the first female picador.

There is an anti-bullfighting pressure group in Spain, but it receives little attention. Those who fondly imagine that Brussels will exert its influence against a member state which continues to indulge in the savage torture and killing of innocent animals overlook the fact that bullfights are very popular in south-west France. Bull rings are to be found up the Mediterranean coast as far as Arles and, on the Atlantic side, all over the Basque country, to within forty miles of Bordeaux.

Spanish matadors, who respect the French crowds, enjoy visiting French rings, where the fight is conducted precisely as it is in Spain. True, in France it is technically illegal to kill a bull in the ring; but this is not something that the French take too seriously. The payment of a nominal fine on each occasion to the municipal authority seems to satisfy everyone.

Some French rings offer a double bill – a *novillada* (with younger bulls and apprentice matadors) in the morning, and a *corrida* in the afternoon; and about a hundred and twenty fights take place in France during the season. It is ironic that there is probably more *afición* in parts of what was once French Catalonia than in the Spanish province of Catalonia, where they tend to look down on bullfighting as being rather uncivilised, a pastime which really belongs to those primitive people in Andalusia. Barcelona, however, does have the second largest bullring in Spain.

It would be too simplistic to say that Catalans are anti-bullfighting; it is just that they like to consider themselves superior to, and different from, other Spaniards. Where there is opposition to bullfighting in Spain, things are unlikely to be as straightforward as they may appear. Animal rights and ecological groups across Europe were quick to proclaim the mayor of Tossa as a hero when he banned bullfights from his town on the Costa Brava in 1989; but they looked foolish when the circumstances became known. It was not so much a principled stand against a barbarous practice as a cautionary tale of the Spanish character.

The mayor was a tough old fisherman who did not always get on with the councillor responsible for developing tourism in this popular coastal resort. At meetings the councillor kept on insisting that Tossa needed to hold more bullfights, but the mayor thought there were quite enough already. The argument continued until one day he became so exasperated by the councillor raising the matter at a meeting yet again that, in order to shut him up, the mayor got to his feet and announced that he would put a stop to all bullfights in Tossa.

The mayor was later happy to admit that his concern for the welfare of the bulls was not uppermost in his mind at the time. But, as he said when he became famous in animal protection circles, a man can change his views – especially when he is getting such good publicity for his town.

One of the charges levelled at Spaniards is that they delight in being cruel to animals – which is untrue. They simply regard humans and animals in a different light, and the death of a Spanish fighting bull by a matador's sword as something which can ennoble both man and beast. The beast in question is a truly remarkable animal, bred over the centuries to attack on sight and destroy whatever appears to threaten its territory. When it has been matched in the ring with a lion or elephant, the bull has always been the clear winner. At the start of a *corrida* it charges the cape, which appears the better target, and because it has never seen a man on foot before. But after twenty minutes, when it is about to die, the bull can no longer be fooled. No matador in his right mind would let the bull live to fight again.

Those who would rather that the fighting bull did no fighting must accept the inevitability that the breed would then face certain extinction. Bull breeders would have no other use for the animal, because it is not good at converting grass into protein. Rather than switch to other breeds of beef cattle, however, they would be more likely to turn the land over to flower and vegetable production under glass and plastic. The wildlife which now flourishes in those areas grazed by fighting bulls would be destroyed.

This chapter is not intended as a defence of bullfighting but rather as an account of its place in the life of Spain. (Significantly, perhaps, funerals and *corridas* are the only two events in Spain which can be relied on to start on time.) The spectacle can be disappointing, shameful, repellent, fascinating, stimulating, moving and sometimes plain boring. Perhaps I can best illustrate my own reactions by reference to two *toreros* – Antonio Ordoñez, the *numero uno* of his time in the 1950s and 1960s, and an extraordinary contemporary of his, Curro Romero, who was still fighting, aged sixty-three, in 1997.

Though bullfighting is not a sport, Ordoñez can legitimately be compared with sportsmen such as Lester Piggott and Jack Nicklaus who were at the top of their professions for two decades and more. In the ring he sometimes reminded me of the great baritone Tito Gobbi: the swagger and style were not dissimilar and each had and enjoyed displaying the authority of someone who knew how good he was.

I don't know what sort of man Gobbi was; but Ordoñez was not an attractive character outside the ring. He was said to have belonged to an extreme right-wing political party, Fuerza Nueva, in the sixties; and I was glad not to have witnessed an incident related to me by a friend who had spent several seasons following Ordoñez round Spain. In a bar after a fight in Seville, Ordoñez, flanked by a couple of assistants, approached a bullfight critic of one of the Madrid papers

94

and proceeded to abuse him and physically assault him because he had been less than generous about one of Ordoñez's recent performances in the ring. However, it is surely irrelevant how a great performer behaves after the show. Vanessa Redgrave's attachment to the Workers' Revolutionary party and her support for the Palestine Liberation Organisation have never diminished for me her wondrous qualities as an actress.

Antonio Ordoñez had, in the words of Kenneth Tynan in *Bull Fever*, 'a wholly lyric talent'. In the fifties and sixties he was a cult figure among English and American aficionados. Certainly Hemingway had something to do with it – by his public patronage of Ordoñez in 1959 in preference to his great rival, Luis Miguel Dominguin – and I can remember being in the house of a friend of Hemingway's in Andalusia where all the talk was of Antonio, his recent triumphs and his forthcoming programme. He had been brilliant in Valencia; we must be sure not to miss him in Bilbao.

We were, I suppose, 'groupies' in the way some of us followed the fortunes of Ordoñez, on occasion driving overnight from one town to another, as he was doing, in order to watch him perform the next afternoon. As he paraded with the others across the ring (pausing always in the middle to scuff his feet in the sand, rather as a bull will paw the ground), and doffed his *montera* to reveal the slicked black hair and those swarthy, aristocratically confident features, the excitement began again. And what was it that set Ordoñez apart from the rest? Hemingway wrote that Ordoñez used a cape 'as no one alive had ever used it'. He did have a classical fluency of style, drawing the bull past his body as if in slow motion, which could give to his performances an emotional thrill which no other matador of the time was able to match.

In 1980, twenty years after I first saw him, I made the mistake of going to see Ordoñez fight one more time. By then he was nearly fifty, had already retired several times, but couldn't resist a few more appearances in the ring. Stopping at a hotel before the fight, I saw Ordoñez in the foyer, dressed in his matador's 'suit of lights'. He had a paunch, was limping and looked badly out of condition. In the bullring he was greeted by a standing ovation but it was soon apparent that the magic had gone – or he wasn't trying – and before long he was being jeered and cushions were being thrown. Though all bullfighters have their share of bad days, I wished I hadn't witnessed this one.

Ten years later, passing through Ordoñez's home town of Ronda, I stopped to visit the bullfighting museum. There were photographs of the great man in action, photographs of him with Orson Welles and with Hemingway, and of his father, who was the model for the matador in *The Sun Also Rises*. I also learnt that Ordoñez had fought for the last time in the annual festival in Ronda in September 1980, a few weeks after I had seen him. A waiter in a nearby bar confirmed that it had been a magnificent and truly memorable farewell performance. Though I did not really expect him to tell me that Ronda's favourite son had been embarrassingly awful, I was grateful to hear what he said, and went happily on my way.

It was at that house in Andalusia, where the Ordoñez groupies used to gather, that I once met Curro Romero. A delightful American couple, Bill and Annie Davis, used to keep open house for an assortment of gamblers, writers and lay-abouts at La Consula, their villa near Malaga. Romero had come to lunch, and during the afternoon was invited to play poker. I tried unsuccessfully to explain to him the 'high-low' version of the game – *arriba abajo* did not quite seem to cover it – but, as I remember, he played, and bluffed, with aplomb. He was a purist in the ring, I was told: he did not often give a good performance, but the few were worth waiting for. He was the bullfighters' bullfighter.

I never saw him fight during those years, indeed had all but forgotten the name of Curro Romero, until the spring of 1992, when I was in Seville and saw that he was due to fight on two consecutive days. It was worth checking first that this was the same Curro Romero whom I had met thirty years ago. No doubt of that: he was still a hero in Seville, *insustituible*, according to the manager of the Maestranza bullring. No *feria* could take place without him. It is hard to explain the adulation that Curro Romero was still enjoying in Seville in the mid-1990s, though he fought no more than a dozen times during a season. He receives something akin to pop-star treatment from his fans, who are known as *curristas*. They are part of the cult of *currismo*, and many wear a sprig of rosemary (*romero*) in their buttonholes. Curro's credentials, too, are impeccable: as an Andalusian with no doubt a good dose of Moorish or gypsy blood in his veins, he is known as El Faraon de Camas – referring to his supposedly Egyptian style (whatever that may mean) and to the village of his birth. A gypsy is said to have told him: 'I hate your fear, which is my fear; I love your art, which is my art. Sun and shade of a passionate relationship.'

I went to the second of Curro's appearances in the Seville bullring, also attended by the Queen Mother, Doña Maria de las Mercedes, la Condesa de Barcelona. The whole *corrida* was disappointing, largely due to the weakness of the bulls, but when the maestro attempted a few passes, lasting about fifteen seconds, the ring erupted with shouts of '*Olé Currrrr-o!*' In a street bar afterwards a policeman enquired whether I had seen the 'great art of Curro' in those passes, and a waiter tried to reproduce them with his drying-up cloth. And what about yesterday? How could I have missed it? Curro was *estupendísimo*.

What had I missed? The accounts in the Seville papers raved on, for column after column, about the maestro's triumph. 'The inspired art of Curro was like the famous light of Seville,' was one headline. The way in which he fought his second bull 'will leave in its wake a light which will shine at least until the year 2000'. It was irresistible stuff, from which one might have expected that Curro would have been given the bull's ears (awarded by the president of the ring for an outstanding performance), if not the tail and one or two hooves as well. However, he received nothing, as he had failed to kill the bull cleanly, which is, after all, what the matador is employed to do. Yet, according to one less than impartial reporter, 'in the case of Curro, it doesn't count'.

I consulted Michael Wigram, one of the most respected and objective of bullfight critics, who writes a column for the Madrid magazine, *6 Toros 6*. He had been at that first corrida and did not share his colleagues' views. 'You missed nothing,' he told me. 'There were middle-aged men screaming with excitement all around me, yet Curro did nothing more than make a few easy passes with a bull that had been crippled by his picadors. It was a ridiculous exhibition.' Wigram used to be *currista* himself in the sixties and seventies, when Curro was a great artist, even though increasingly rarely seen at his best. But now he had become a pathetic caricature: in Madrid he has been known to leave the ring protected from the missiles of an angry crowd by riot police covering him with plastic shields.

But in Seville he is a legend. Perhaps the Sevillan newspaper critics do not need to indulge in quite such a surfeit of hyperbole, but they would not keep their jobs if they started questioning Curro's genius. Even when he does nothing, he is described as doing it 'with dignity and grace, at his own inimitable pace'. The taurine correspondent of the tabloid *ABC* in Seville, Vicente Zabala (who was killed in an air crash at the end of 1995), was one of those who appreciated the importance of being *currista*. Were he not, he might have lost not only his job but the friendship of the Duchess of Alba and the valued invitations to her private box at the annual fair after Easter.

Curro's influential followers are not confined to Seville. Joaquin Vidal, the senior taurine critic of the leading Madrid newspaper *El Pais*, takes the view that the *corrida* can only be justified as an art, as occasionally or formerly exhibited by Curro Romero. Most modern matadors are dismissed by Vidal as 'professionals'. A book published in 1987, *The Enigma of Curro Romero*, was dedicated to 'those who have never seen him fight'. (Some may cynically ask, 'Are they the lucky ones?') It is arguable whether they would want to after reading passages such as this: 'Curro Romero is a landmark, a singular and profound phenomenon in the history of bullfighting because he is, perhaps, the matador who with the greatest rigour places fear against art, love against hate, the instant against memory, technique against miracle, existential concepts against aesthetic concepts, ethical concepts against philosophical concepts.'

Even his greatest fans might be unaware that he did all these things while doing his best to avoid getting caught by the bull. More perceptively, the book comments that 'people go to see Curro Romero for much the same reason as they buy lottery tickets'. He may occasionally have provided the big pay-out over the past three decades, but not any more. The real enigma is how Curro can go on getting away with it. Presumably the old boy still has some style, but the cult status of his reputation in the capital city of the south is something of a mystery.

In 1994 he was receiving around eight million pesetas (over £40,000) for an afternoon's work. Since in recent years he has done little with the cape and has invariably killed badly, that is a lot of pesetas for the outside chance of a few passes with the red cloth during a short *faena*. By this time he will have ensured, by specific instructions to the picadors, that the bull is probably too weak to put up a fight. It is hard to resist the conclusion that, after all those years since we once played poker together, Curro Romero has become a master of bluff.

If Curro Romero is the last of the old guard, as he assuredly is, Jesulin de Ubrique, forty years his junior, very much represents the new. In his outrageous yellow *traje de luces*, he seems to be almost constantly on television – whether in the bullring, giving interviews or appearing in a commercial with a tiger on his lap. Although he fights more often than any other matador, Jesulin is not generally considered the best. That accolade is hotly contested by Enrique Ponce and Jose Miguel Arroyo, known as Joselito, though Ordonez's young grandson, Francisco Rivera Ordonez, is snapping at their heels. Joselito, having named himself, somewhat arrogantly, after perhaps the most famous bullfighter of all time, seems to be bearing comparison with his *soi-disant* mentor and forbear. The original Joselito, a *sevillano* born in 1895, was truly a phenomenon. He had his first professional fight at the age of thirteen, and at seventeen, though still an apprentice, he fought full-sized, five-year-old bulls in Madrid. For six years from 1914, he and his rival Belmonte fought together in what came to be known as the Golden Age of bullfighting. But by 1920 their public began to tire of their performances: they were consistently too good, they seemed almost to have eliminated the element of risk and Joselito, in particular, appeared invulnerable, incapable of ever being caught by the bull. On 15 May 1920, at the end of a *corrida* in Madrid, a woman was heard to shout at Joselito: 'I hope a bull kills you tomorrow in Talavera.'

And so it was to be. A small bull, with defective vision, gored him in the right thigh, then with the other horn ripped open his stomach. Within two hours Joselito, a week after his twenty-fifth birthday, was dead. The monument on his tomb in Seville, sculpted by Mariano Benlliure, depicts nineteen life-sized figures in bronze – weeping gypsies, bull breeders and matadors – bearing the body of their hero.

The bullring at Talavera de la Reina stands on the outskirts of the undistinguished town, seventy miles west of Madrid, which was the site of one of Wellington's victories. Next to the ring is the Basílica de Nuestra Señora de Prado and, between them, a little avenue dedicated to Joselito and inscribed with the date of his death, 16 May 1920. I pushed open the Puerta de Cuadrillas and walked past the stables for the picadors' horses to find an old lady hanging out her washing in a small courtyard grown over with moss. She took me to the entrance to the ring and pointed across the sand. 'That's where he fell,' she said; 'between *tendidos* 1 and 2, about five metres from the *barrera*.' We walked over to the spot and stood for a moment in silence. Above the empty rows of seats were placards advertising Citroen and Nissan cars, and beyond the bullring a stork was nesting on the church tower.

SEVEN

English Connections

In a country that has known so much violence throughout its history, it may be invidious to claim that one region has experienced more savagery and murder than any other. But I would unhesitatingly nominate Estremadura – so called, I used to think, because life in this poor and largely infertile region can be 'extremely hard'. The name is in fact taken from the Latin, *extrema ora*: this was the last (extreme) conquest of Alfonso IX, who finally drove out the Moors in the thirteenth century.

The land was extensively cultivated by the Romans, and later under the Moorish occupation. Agriculture was neglected, however, once the Estremenians were left on their own, and they soon relapsed into poverty and indolence, until the temptation to enrich themselves in the New World became irresistible. But the conquistadors of Estremadura, for all their deeds of derring-do in Mexico and Peru, were a pretty barbaric lot, even by the standards of the sixteenth century. They would train their dogs to kill Indians, rewarding the animals with some of their booty. (Nuñez de Balboa who, like Cortes, came from Medellin on the Guadiana river, owned a famously rich killer dog named Leoncico. When his master was executed, the dog apparently stood for days howling up at the post on which Balboa's head was staked.)

Passing over, for a moment, the suffering endured by Estremadura during the Peninsular War, the continuous conflict between large absentee landowners and landless peasants, from the eighteenth cen-

tury onwards, had reached a point by the 1930s where anarchism and mass violence were inevitable. More than three thousand estates were forcibly taken over by some sixty thousand labourers in the province of Badajoz and collective farming was introduced. Though the village massacre at Castilblanco (see page 34), near Guadalupe, at the end of 1931 was an extreme illustration of the behaviour of the people of this still wild and inhospitable region, it can be attributed in part to their poverty, revolutionary fervour and to Estremadura's violent history.

Several cities in Spain can lay claim (should they wish to do so) to bloody pasts; but surely none would come closer to the top of the historical league table of brutality than Badajoz. Ever since it was wrested from the Moors, Elizabeth Longford wrote in her biography of Wellington, 'Badajoz had earned a reputation for strength through blood'.

O, Nelly Gray! O, Nelly Gray!
For all your jeering speeches,
At duty's call, I left my legs
In Badajos's breaches!

Thomas Hood's 'pathetic ballad' of Ben Battle was not one of the poems that I read at school; but many did. Gerald Brenan recalled the 'queer, far-off, schoolboy memories' of Badajoz. 'The boring classroom and the smug tone of the history master's voice as he spoke of its sack by Wellington's troops – the pun in Thomas Hood's poem, printed in a little red school edition that cost sixpence – the look of the name itself, so absurd in its English pronunciation!'

Ben Battle was a soldier bold,
And used to war's alarms;
But a cannon-ball took off his legs,
So he laid down his arms!

This blackly humorous poem ends with Ben Battle hanging himself, because Faithless Nelly Gray refused to have a legless lover. But at least he had survived the siege of Badajoz – which claimed the lives of nearly five thousand British troops and reduced Wellington to tears. It was the third attempt to take the city, which finally fell during the night of 6–7 April 1812. With the help of a large number of *afrancesados* (French sympathisers) among the Spanish inhabitants, General Philippon had had plenty of time to fortify the castle and its approaches with ingenious deterrents – including planks studded with spikes and Toledo steel sword-blades. One soldier's account described how, during the storming of the fortress, 'from the very earth destruction burst, for the exploding mines cast up friends and foes together, who in burning torture slashed and shrieked in the air.'

The British troops entered Badajoz around midnight, and they began to sack it. In Elizabeth Longford's chilling description, 'Sudden release from one hell only plunged them into another. Every door was battered in, old men were shot, women raped, children bayoneted.'

Frighteningly similar atrocities were to occur in Badajoz a hundred and twenty-four years later when the Army of Africa, advancing north during the first weeks of the civil war, breached the same walls that had been defended by the French in 1812. The looting and carnage were indiscriminate, much of it committed by Moroccan troops who, when not restrained, indulged in the traditional Moorish battle-rite – castrating the corpses of their victims. Contemporary accounts, from 1936 as from 1812, indicate that neither commander, having taken Badajoz, intervened to stop the killings. Wellington waited until the following day to order 'that the plunder of Badajoz should cease', and argued later that, had he put the garrison of Ciudad Rodrigo to the sword the year before, he would have saved five thousand lives at Badajoz.

Colonel Yagüe, who commanded the *legionarios* and Moorish *regulares* that formed the Army of Africa, was reported as saying, 'Of course we shot them. Was I expected to turn them loose in my rear and let them make Badajoz Red again?' Instead he made the bullring red by herding nearly two thousand militiamen and other citizens into the arena and massacring them. Elsewhere in the city republicans were pursued even into the cathedral, where fighting took place on the altar steps.

Just inside the Puerta de la Trinidad, which was stormed by the fourth bandera of the Foreign Legion shouting their battle cry, '*Viva la Muerte!*', it is ironic to find today an area of gardens named Parque de la Legion. Next to it a new bullring has been built; the old one was surrounded by a high wire fence at the end of 1994, barring access, it seemed, to the guilty secret of its past. Before the sixtieth anniversary of the massacre, however, the bullring was due to be demolished and landscaped for building plots, at a cost of thirty million pesetas.

Behind the ring, and at two other points in Badajoz, the remains of the seventeenth-century walls face outwards over what were then the approaches to the city. But today the only view from the walls is of featureless apartment blocks, with sheets hanging out to dry on their flat roofs and a maze of television aerials. A graffito on one of the old walls reads, depressingly, *'Todo muere— Viva a l'Utopia!'*

The cathedral, in the centre of the old city, has a tower that looks not unlike an English parish church. It is surrounded by narrow streets where one can easily imagine that, during the two sackings of Badajoz, local residents were trapped and murdered or raped. Many of the houses off the cathedral square have attractive windows, with wrought-iron or glass-covered balconies, and decorative plasterwork above the lintels. In the Calle de General Menacho the headquarters of the military governor stand, perhaps appropriately, facing a convent.

The recent expansion of Badajoz may have been inevitable but, seen from across the Guadiana river, the rows of 1960s tower blocks serve only to disfigure the landscape at the western end of the city. A few miles over the border into Portugal, it is very noticeable that the town of Elvas – also the site of one of Wellington's battles – remains almost entirely confined within its old walls.

No memorial to Wellington is visible in Badajoz (though I was glad to see a Peninsula supermarket on the Portuguese border); but the height of the fortress walls, and the steepness of the grass banks approaching them, still bear impressive witness to the daring and the remarkable achievement of Wellington's troops on that night. Among the old fortifications of the Alcazaba today is a military hospital; and at one end of a makeshift football pitch, fringed with palm trees and cypresses, there stands a sprawling stone monument, presumably to the siege, but with no inscription other than the scratched names and initials of countless visitors.

I returned to the castle at night, when the battlements were silhouetted against a full moon appearing from behind cloud. Traffic police trucks with cranes were bringing illegally parked cars up the hill to a pound within the gates of the military hospital (this seems to be a favourite police pastime in Badajoz). Standing on the ramparts, I looked down on the lights of cars flashing by on either side of the Guadiana river, where in 1812 the same scene was illuminated by the

105

flash of exploding shells. From across the river I could hear – it was no flight of fancy – the beat of what sounded like regimental drums.

When George Borrow crossed the Spanish frontier in 1836, he entered Badajoz by the sixteenth-century bridge of thirty arches known as the Puente de Palmas. The banks of the Guadiana, he wrote in *The Bible in Spain*, 'were white with linen which the washerwomen had spread out to dry in the sun . . . I heard their singing at a great distance, and the theme seemed to be the praises of the river where they were toiling'.

V. S. Pritchett came here in 1928, walking his way northwards to Vigo. He too crossed the same bridge, on which 'the donkeys and mules increased and the songs with them. A gypsy was singing in his shack by the river.' When I walked across the bridge, there were donkeys grazing near the eucalyptus groves on the riverbank, and, closer to the road, allotments growing cactus and spinach beet. Two black cranes flew overhead. An old woman in black was on her knees near the river, gathering what appeared to be grass and stuffing it into a plastic sack, watched by two mongrel dogs. But, unlike the washerwomen and the gypsies, she was not singing. 'Nobody sings in Spain any more,' I was told in a bar that evening. 'I can remember the days when you would always hear people singing in the streets or at work; but not now. Television is to blame.'

In the middle of the bridge are two turrets, leaning slightly like children's bouncing castles. At the far end you pass through the Puerta de Palmas, flanked by a pair of squat towers, which gives entrance to the city. Sentries and officials were stationed at the gate when Borrow and Pritchett walked through. Nowadays the first sight to greet the visitor, having passed under the arch, is a newsstand bedecked with pornographic magazines.

In the nineteenth century Borrow found Badajoz full of gypsies, to whom he tried to preach the gospel; and here he embarked on a translation of the New Testament into the Spanish gypsy tongue. Pritchett commented, nearly a hundred years later, that the city was 'as oriental as Tunis. It was little more than an Arab kasbah . . . Every doorstep had its trade. There were carpenters, smiths, wheelwrights, cart makers, basket makers . . . and a procession of donkeys carrying cans of milk, or baskets of oranges like red-hot coals, or a struggling sack of chickens tied together in bunches by the legs.' None of this is evident today, although there are plenty of swarthy faces to be seen among the young footballers on top of the old castle walls.

Pritchett's greatest surprise in Badajoz was to find a Protestant Scottish minister living there, with a wife made miserable by being continually abused and persecuted by the local people, who referred to their home as the House of Ill Fame. He had, however, managed to convert a handful to the Protestant faith.

Religious intolerance continued over much of Spain for some years, and it was not until 1967 that Protestants were allowed to be buried in a Spanish municipal cemetery. For this reason the British government would, from time to time, purchase plots of land for the interring of its citizens who died in Spain. The oldest, and largest, is to be found in Malaga.

Across the street from the bullring, opposite the Centre for Aesthetics and Massages and next to an ironmonger's shop, two lions, each with a paw resting on a globe, guard the gates to the English Cemetery. Beyond the Victorian lodge, with gabled roof and Gothic windows, some three acres of garden are laid out, against the steep hillside rising to the Gibralfaro. Here are headstones, tombstones, memorials and monuments to the English residents of the province of Malaga – and to a number of German sailors and the occasional American and Hungarian ambassador.

In 1829 the then British consul was granted this piece of land by the governor of the city and took possession of it 'in the name of King George the Fourth for ever'. It is not some corner of a foreign field: it is British territory, shaded by cypresses and palm trees, and surrounded by hedges of bougainvillaea and myrtle. But there are fears for its future.

Dark rumours have been circulating among the 'expat' community along this southern coast that we are in danger of losing our cemetery. Is nothing sacred? It is not so much the possibility of compulsory purchase by the city authorities – though this could become a real threat under a less anglophile mayor – as the continuing cost of maintaining the cemetery.

While the official line is that the local community is responsible for the upkeep of the cemetery and the Foreign Office has no intention of selling it, it is British government property and, if local funds run out, a decision will have to be taken whether, from the Foreign Office's ever-shrinking budget, the taxpayer should keep the cemetery going. The general feeling here is that the Foreign Office would prefer to be shot of it, and to realise its very valuable asset close to the city centre.

Local financial support is hardly overwhelming. A determined fund-raising effort, using local television and newspapers, raised just under £1,000. 'We need a burial a month to pay for the cemetery and we're not getting enough bodies,' was how one resident put it. The charge for a burial is about £1,100; the only other income comes from the sale of a few plants and shrubs.

On the expenditure side there is Pepe, the rather mournful-looking gardener with a drooping moustache and a black mongrel dog. He lives in the lodge with his father, Antonio, who proudly shows off his MBE, for devoted gardening services to the British consulate. However, repairs to the fabric of the cemetery – part of one arm of the cross on the wall of the inner burial ground is missing – tend to be overlooked.

At one end of the cemetery garden stands a Greek Revival sandstone lodge-temple, which was built in 1840 and converted into St George's Church in 1891. This church is in the unusual position of having an adjacent burial-ground which does not belong to it. The Foreign Office would rather not be in the business of running cemeteries; it would gladly hand this one over to the Church, rather as the consulate in Naples did a few years ago with Christ Church, for which it used to be responsible. But the Anglican Church in Europe (the diocese of the Bishop of Gibraltar in Europe) has not got the money. The Church Commissioners give no financial assistance to overseas chaplains, whose stipends and expenses have to come from generous parishioners.

There is no shortage of English money around Malaga – some of it, along the notorious Costa del Crime, from ill-gotten gains – but not much gets diverted to the local English chaplain. Nor are large sums likely to be given to the cemetery. Of the many thousands of 'expats', about thirty-five people attend Sunday services at St George's, though donations come from a larger number. The current chaplain, the Reverend Bill Pegg, lives in a flat bequeathed by a naval commander's widow who died five years ago.

The future of the English Cemetery could be assured if a large benefactor came forward – perhaps a refugee from British justice anxious to transfer some of his treasure to heaven. An increase in the rate of deaths and the number of burials would also help. One would have thought there were plenty of retired couples around here, in the very late evening of their lives, who would prefer to be interred in this beautiful place rather than have their bodies returned, much more expensively, to Britain. (Many are cremated here, which saves a lot of money on transport.)

As one walks round the cemetery, it is hard to believe that anyone – even the British Government – would disturb this oasis of peace. Lancashire voices were plainly audible as two elderly ladies passed by, one of them wearing pale slacks and carrying flowers. They paused to peer into a large hole, a grave in waiting, which is the custom in Spain. Some of the graves, covered in cockle-shells, are of children who died of malaria in the last century. Sixty-two officers and men of the Imperial German Navy were buried here in a common grave when the training ship *Gneisenau* sank outside the harbour in 1900. Four war graves stand together, the bodies recovered from the sea during the second world war. There are several memorials to Americans here; and 'tucked away in one corner', Jan Morris found the grave of a solitary Jew some years ago.

Geraniums grow by the memorial to William Mark, 'consul for the kingdom of Granada at Malaga', who persuaded the Malaga authorities to grant the land for the burial of British subjects. Years before, he had observed 'with great grief and disgust' the bodies of Protestants being taken to the beach 'at the dead hour of midnight' and buried in the sand, apparently upright and facing the sea. Rubbish and ordure were often dumped around their resting places.

If the heirs of William Mark decline to use any taxpayers' money and, without enough local money to support it, decide to sell the English Cemetery, some of the remains may have to go back to the beach. In England certain procedures have to be followed if the Church Commissioners want to dispose of a churchyard. Similar regulations govern the disposal of a cemetery by a local authority, under the Town and Country Planning Act – which presumably the British consul would have to observe.

All human remains must be removed and reinterred before a cemetery is deconsecrated and sold, and notices must be published to allow time for the remains and tombstones to be removed by relatives. Any that are still there after two months must be taken away and reburied by 'the person in whom the land is vested'.

Unlike a churchyard or other burial-ground in Britain, the cemetery in Malaga contains very few graves of people with relatives living in the neighbourhood. Notices in local newspapers – even in *Sur in English* – would bring very little response. The British consul would, therefore, be faced with having to remove the vast majority of human remains, not to mention the tombstones and other memorials. What, one wonders, would he do with them all? Would other consecrated ground be made available in the vicinity? Or would the remains have to be reinterred, with those of earlier English Protestants, in the sand along the Mediterranean shore?

In the north corner of the cemetery I came upon a grave recently filled; no turf had been placed over the top, but cement had been laid just below ground level. So that is the practice of Spanish grave-diggers: the bodies are entombed beneath a layer of concrete. This should surely be enough to save the English Cemetery from desecration and development.

The church itself is a friendly building, extended in 1967 to provide a stained glass window behind the altar, with its striking modern tableau of the Last Supper. On the north wall of the church, halfway down the aisle, a St George window commemorates Admiral Henry Wilkin, 'who entered into fuller life at Malaga, 8.1.31'. In the vestry the visit in 1927 of Princess Beatrice, youngest daughter of Queen Victoria, is recorded.

Either Matins (Book of Common Prayer) or Holy Communion (Rite B) is celebrated every Sunday morning at St George's, with a congregation that may include Germans and Scandinavians, and even a South American. A few miles down the coast at Torremolinos, a Saturday evening service is held in the basement bar of the Bajondillo Hotel, using an Irish hymnal and taped music. Several of the congregation, at least in winter, are elderly Americans. The Reverend Bill Pegg estimates that about two thirds of his congregations are over seventy-five; much of his time is spent in visiting his parishioners in hospital. Nowadays their treatment will be paid for by the National Health Service (so long as they can produce the relevant form, E1–11). But the lack of nursing aftercare, or 'home help' – because in Spain the caring is done within the family – can cause problems for elderly convalescent Brits living on their own.

At Los Boliches, next to Fuengirola, where the chaplaincy is held by the Reverend Trevor Devamanikkam, the oldies were crowding in to St Andrew's Church on a weekday morning. They had not come to worship, but to gossip and drink coffee in what they referred to as the church hall. A photograph on the wall of King Juan Carlos looked benignly on this curious gathering, where most of the accents were north country – Manchester, not Bilbao. A charity shop was being run in one corner of the hall, from which the church pews and altar were screened off. St Andrew's was converted from a shop, standing next to an apartment block and a Finnish café, and facing the railway line which runs above the road. Along the coast, east and west of Malaga, Catholic churches may be used for Anglican services, and good relations are maintained with the local Spanish priests.

Whatever the future of the English Cemetery, access will surely always be granted for worshippers to walk from the road to St George's church. Looking at a mid-nineteenth-century print of the lodge-temple flanked by rows of tall cypresses, I had a horrible impression for a moment of how the church might look were the trees to be replaced by apartment blocks. If the English Cemetery is ever itself buried under concrete, one will have to look much farther afield for memorials to Britons who died in Spain.

Most of them are military, from the early nineteenth century. Apart from Moore's grave at Corunna (see page 29), there is a British naval cemetery outside Villagarcia in Galicia, established when warships of the Royal Navy used the bay as a base for excursions into the Atlantic.

It stands next to the municipal cemetery and the Buenos Aires garage. Then there is a charming small cemetery which I came upon recently in San Sebastian.

The British Auxiliary Legion was fighting around San Sebastian during the first Carlist War of 1836–7. Some of those who died were buried in what is known as the English Cemetery, on the far side of Mount Urgull, looking not on to the bay and beach of La Concha but northwards out across the Bay of Biscay towards Britain. Climbing the steep hill past granite boulders, bracken and tamarisk, I was momentarily reminded of Cornwall, but it was too hot for the impression to last. Samphire, thrift and vetch also grow on this peaceful hillside quite hidden from the city. The group of gravestones and headstones – standing not far below the giant statue of the Virgin which dominates the top of Mount Urgull – is shaded by pine trees and surrounded by pink hydrangeas and euonymus bushes, with some very British brambles growing out of them.

It is perhaps inevitable that the Spanish plan of the burial-ground fails to correspond with the actual position and number of headstones. And it is enjoyably ironic to find that the largest memorial, in what is called El Cementerio de los Ingleses, is to a Scotsman. The inscription reads:

Sacred to the memory of
Whiliam [*sic*] I. M. Tupper,
Colonel of the 6° Scotch BAL
and late of the 23° RWE,
who at the head of his reg°
at the taking of Ayete
on the 5 May 1836
fell mortally wounded
at 32 years of age.

It is repeated in Spanish on the other side of the stone.

The memorial to 'John Callander Esq, lately inspector general of hospitals', has an inscription referring to his wife and daughter; but most of it is no longer legible. The plan of the cemetery marks the grave of Colonel Sir Richard Fletcher, but unfortunately I could find

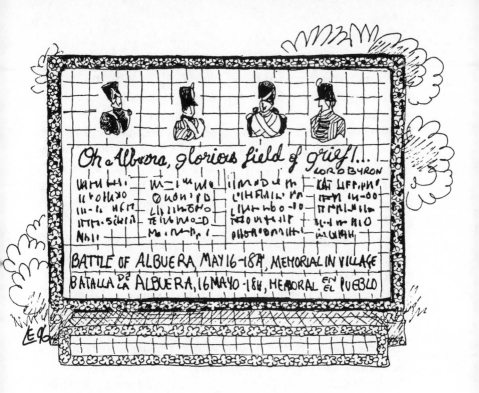

Oh Albuera, glorious field of grief!...
LORD BYRON

BATTLE OF ALBUERA, MAY 16-18ª, MEMORIAL IN VILLAGE
BATALLA DE LA ALBUERA, 16 MAYO-18ᵘ, MEMORAL EN EL PUEBLO

no trace of it. It was Fletcher who, at the siege of Badajoz, was famously hit by a bullet which struck his sporran, forcing a silver dollar into his groin but otherwise doing no damage to the gallant colonel. He was to meet his death the following year at the siege of San Sebastian, when Wellington's troops, 'the very scum of the earth', sacked and effectively destroyed the city.

It comes as a surprise, therefore, to find the British role in the Peninsular War commemorated in a museum in the old quarter of San Sebastian. Engravings depict the Iron Duke and British redcoats fighting the French in the Pyrenees. The British volunteers who helped in the defence of San Sebastian in 1836 went some way to atoning for the shameful episode of 1813; and in the later years of the century anglophilia was much in evidence.

The Queen Regent, Maria Cristina, employed an English architect to build the egregious Palacio de Miramar, a wonderfully absurd mock-Tudor, mock-Gothic pile standing prominently above the bay.

The mixture of red brick, stone mullioned windows, gabled dormers, black-and-white timbered tower, stained oak veranda and balcony, and partly castellated facade would be considered excessive even in the 'stockbroker belt' of the Home Counties. In San Sebastian it is ludicrously out of place – even though the Hotel Londres y Inglaterra is only a few hundred yards away along the front. Up the hill behind the city, the Palacio de Ayete, a grand 'French' house of the 1870s, was also built by Maria Cristina and visited by Queen Victoria, according to a plaque on a monument in the garden, on 27 March 1889. She was the first reigning British monarch ever to set foot in Spain – two years after the birth of her granddaughter Victoria Eugenie (Ena), who would marry Maria Cristina's son, King Alfonso XIII, in 1906.

The historical English connection is hard to find in Spain. H. V. Morton wrote that 'you could travel all over Spain without realising that British armies under the Duke of Wellington fought there during the Peninsular War'. This is not quite true: plaques are to be found in Salamanca and Ciudad Rodrigo, and in Vitoria a fine statue of a British lion clawing a French eagle (a satisfying image for today's opponents of European Union). Outside Talavera de la Reina a monument to Wellington stands by the main road; but in the town itself I could find no one who had heard of him or of the battle. Eventually someone directed me to the Calle Duque de Wellington, a miserable, narrow street of houses with barred windows and five-storey blocks with their blinds drawn in mid-January. The gloomy harmony of the artificial brick buildings was relieved only by a heating engineer's shop and a bar, *El Emigrante*. Round the corner in the Calle Santa Teresa de Jesus and celebrating, I liked to think, the country of Wellington's birth, was the *Taberna El Irlandes*.

Only at La Albuera is the Peninsular War properly commemorated. Whether you approach this Estremaduran village of low, white-walled houses from Badajoz or from Zafra, the memorial tablets on the main road are impossible to miss. Here are Byron's words from *Childe Harold's Pilgrimage*, 'Oh Albuera, glorious field of grief!', impressions of soldiers painted on white tiles from the armies of Spain, Britain, France and Portugal and, in their four languages, the moving words:

'In rows, just like they fought, they lay like the hay in the open countryside when the night falls and the mower falls silent. That is how they were slain.'

Some four thousand of the Allied troops were slain, out of ten thousand; the French, under Soult, lost seven thousand out of twenty-four thousand. In Wellington's absence, General Beresford commanded the victorious forces, but it was a victory won at terrible cost. In the village centre there is a memorial to Generals Castaños, Beresford and Blake in the Plaza de España, and the Calle 16 de Mayo runs into the square. An international ceremony is held here every year on that date, under the auspices of the Wellington Society; it is sometimes attended by representatives from Poland, whose lancers fought with the French at La Albuera.

Because there was not much love lost between the British and Spanish armies during the Peninsular War, it is the more impressive to find such handsome memorial tributes in this otherwise unmemorable village on the plains of Estremadura.

EIGHT

Slow Trains – Fast Deals

At small railway stations in parts of Spain, I have seen notices forbidding blasphemy and foul language. Swearing should certainly be discouraged, at least in public places, but I wonder whether these signs have something to do with the Spaniard's traditional relationship with trains. In his *Wanderings in Spain* (1873), Augustus Hare wrote that the railways were hated and abused and that Spaniards made them go as slowly as possible. 'The train crawls along in the most provoking way, stopping at small stations for two, four, ten, twenty minutes, and giving you ample time to survey the scenery.' When V. S. Pritchett was walking through western Spain in the late 1920s he observed, in *Marching Spain*, that the railway was 'a thing treated no better than a mule or donkey that everyone can ride on, kick and beat as he wishes. The trains are as slow as oxen and as rare as eagles. It is far less surprising to meet a cow or a flock of sheep or a few pigs and chickens on the line than a train.'

Most of the trains in Spain are still slow – if only because they stop so frequently, at the rate of a station every five minutes on some lines – but there are many more of them. I have never actually seen or heard a Spaniard abusing a train, though the condition of station lavatories – even those which you have to pay to use – indicates all too clearly the lack of respect that he shows for railway property.

The first track, on a local line from Barcelona, was laid in 1848. The mainline network across Spain was established by the 1860s, mostly with French financing, and in the early years of this century a narrow-

gauge system was built in those regions, particularly along the north coast, which were not served by the French-owned companies. The railways improved the working-class diet of Madrid in the late nineteenth century by bringing regular supplies of fish to the capital. But the journey remained slow, and by 1930 could no longer compete with lorry transport, even on roads which at that time were usually so rough that much of the fish was probably shaken out of its boxes.

The pace of Spanish train journeys is part of their charm. I am not speaking of the intercontinental or the intercity expresses – such as the 'bullet' train between Madrid and Seville, inaugurated in 1992, which halved the journey time to under three hours – but rather of the cross-country services, used mostly by local people to travel between village and town.

When I first took a Spanish train, described as a *rapido*, in the 1970s, it stopped at every station along the line. Spain must have one of the most comprehensive rail networks in Europe, and surely the largest number of railway stations. Many of them are out in the country, a mile or so from the nearest village, to which they may be connected by no more than a dirt road. Even some large towns, such as Caceres, have stations which are quite a walk from the centre. But if Spanish trains stop a lot, they are, in my experience, reliable and the frequency of local services puts British Rail schedules to shame.

The line from Bilbao via Guernica to the coast at Bermeo is served by trains running every hour, in both directions, throughout the day and on every day of the week. I took a train one Sunday – the service was operating almost every ten minutes – from Madrid to the old university town of Alcalá de Henares, about twenty miles east of the capital. It left from an underground station in the city centre, then passed through one of the main termini on its way out to the depressing suburbs of Vallecas and Vicalvaro. Though it was briefly below ground, this was a proper train – a double-decker with air-conditioning – not to be compared with a London tube train clattering its way from Oxford Circus out to Epping. At Alcalá that evening, the station bookstall was still open and the buffet was, of course, serving *tapas*, alcohol, real coffee and hot milk. Memories of English provincial railway stations on a Sunday are not so sweet.

Scanning my *Horario Guia de Ferrocarriles* – the Bradshaw of the Spanish railway system – I see timetables of so many trips that I long to make. Years ago, I went from Santiago de Compostela to Corunna, then round the coast to El Ferrol – stopping at twenty-nine stations, according to the *horario*, and taking more than three hours. I have still to continue this leisurely journey, along the coast to Gijon, which from El Ferrol can take up to seven and a half hours, stopping at seventy-six stations over a distance of a hundred and ninety miles, at an average speed of twenty-five miles an hour.

But I did take a train at the same sort of average speed, from Oviedo to Santander, a distance of about one hundred and twenty miles. Though we passed through fifty-nine stations along the mostly single-track line, we stopped at only forty-four of them, and the journey took nearly five hours.

This is the narrow-gauge railway, FEVE (Ferrocarriles de Via Estrecha), which winds its picturesque way between the coast and the mountains of the Cordillera Cantabrica; they are sometimes alarmingly close and dramatically high. At the first station, Colloto, we overshot the platform, stopped on a level crossing and reversed; but thereafter the journey proceeded smoothly. I recalled having read somewhere that during the late 1970s Spanish rail accidents had accounted for more deaths than in any other European country; but this may have had something to do with the heady excitement and the liberalising mood of the immediate post-Franco period, which perhaps caused even train drivers or, on one occasion, a bus-driver approaching an unguarded level crossing, to throw caution to the winds.

On we trundled – La Carrera, Pola de Siero, El Remedio (where sheep provided the only sign of life), through Ceceda and Carcanos, where the River Piloña babbled beneath us, to the town of Infiesto, where the railway line seems to form part of the road. I thought for a moment we would have to change trains – since almost everyone seemed to be getting out – but others, mostly elderly couples and a man with a fishing rod, came aboard and we continued our eastward journey.

Small fields of maize and potatoes soon came into view, with much hoeing between the rows by men in dark blue shirts and wide-brimmed, battered straw hats. At Sevares the fisherman got out; below the train window the villagers were haymaking, pitchforking the hay into neat piles while a kestrel hovered above. A little further on, near Arriondas, the hay was being stacked on a horse-drawn cart.

We were by now close to the mountain walls, passing briefly through tunnelled rock and emerging above fast-running rivers, with an occasional distant glimpse of a vulture or some other large bird of prey. Not far up the valley was Covadonga, site of the first battle in which the Spanish succeeded in turning back the Moorish invaders, and the dominating heights of the Picos de Europa.

Around Ribadesella you can just see the sea, if you are looking out for it, but at only one point, after Villahormes, does the train get close to the Atlantic Ocean, running briefly along one of the beaches of the Costa Verde, before turning sharply, as if disapprovingly, inland. But this *costa* is greatly preferable to the one, 'of the Sun', at the bottom of the peninsula.

Between the village halts of Virgen de la Peña and Casar de Peneida (how much more euphonious than Midgham and Thatcham on my local west Berkshire line), the poplars and beeches along the banks of the wide and shallow River Saja recalled for a moment that memorable chapter in *The Sun Also Rises*, when Jake and Bill stop to fish for trout in the Pyrenees on the way to the bulls at Pamplona.

Torrelavega was the only town of any size that we went through, after which the last leg of the journey runs almost parallel to the motorway for a time. We were soon into the industrial suburbs of Santander, only memorable for a station named Boo, neatly complimenting Poo, through which we had passed, near the coast, some two hours before.

I had not had much conversation with my fellow-passengers, most of whom joined the train for less than an hour, but there were few who did not say goodbye as they left. One old man, who got off with me at Santander, and whom I had asked the way to the Hotel Central, insisted on walking there with me. When he told me he had been brought up in Guernica, I marvelled at my luck in meeting someone who had survived the destruction of that town by German bombers in 1937; but it turned out that he had been living in South America during the civil war.

It was on another journey – the stopping train from Barcelona to the French border at the eastern end of the Pyrenees – that I observed several passengers expressing the inalienable right of Spaniards not to do what they are told. In the railway carriage a sign showing a cigarette with a line through it and the words *No Fumar* was prominently displayed. Unconcerned, an old man wearing a blue beret and a young woman in trousers were puffing away, deep in discussion over the cost of housing in this part of Catalonia. The ticket collector passed by without making any protest.

When the train stopped at Figueras, they and other passengers got out and walked across the line, ignoring the sign *No Pasar*. No one bothered to use the subway a little further down the platform, because it was not directly opposite the station exit. How reassuring it was to find such traits of the Spanish character – independence, stubbornness and a distinct whiff of anarchism – surviving the country's radical transformation and democratisation since the death of Franco twenty years ago. And what a relief to know that there are some places where tobacco is still going strong.

I had joined the train at Flassa, three stops north of Gerona, where on a weekday afternoon the station bar was filled with four tables of card-players, all of them smoking and drinking brandy. On one wall the Society for the Protection of Smokers had pinned a notice announcing, 'Mozart was a non-smoker – and he died young.'

Approaching the French frontier – the carriage was almost empty by now, and smoke-free – we crossed rivers and waterfalls, passed rockfaces dotted with cactus and, between tunnels, glimpsed the coastline near Cadaqués. As the train reached its destination at Port-Bou, above the harbour, the Catalan-Talgo express was waiting to cross the frontier, bound for Narbonne, Avignon, Lyon and Geneva. It was an appealing prospect, but I was due in Barcelona by the return train, making more than thirty stops over the three-and-a-half-hour journey.

At most stations, as the train approaches, the man who has been selling tickets leaves his office to play a different and more important role. Grabbing a red flag and a flat-topped red cap, black-peaked and decorated with a silver-leaf cluster, he emerges on to the platform as the station-master. At almost every country halt – except for the smallest, which may be unmanned – the train is greeted by the station-master, who passes the time of day with the driver before seeing the train on its way. As the train pulls out of the station, he can be seen removing his cap and going back to his ticket office. It is a delightful custom, even if it lacks any real practical purpose, other than to check that the train is on time – or thereabouts – and in good working order. Where are the English station-masters of yesteryear?

Every station also records its height above sea level or, more precisely, *sobre el nivel del Mediterraneo en Alicante*. At Camallera, little more than a brick hut with poppies growing through the broken concrete of the platform, the Geographical and Statistical Institute's oval plaque stated that we were eighty-one metres above the Mediterranean; and the *cap d'estacio* (as he called himself, speaking Catalan) saluted smartly, his red flag furled under his left arm, as the train moved off.

Possibly the highest station in Spain – 1236.7 metres above the Mediterranean – is the oddly named Busdongo, between Leon and Oviedo. Here a plaque marks the centenary (1884–1984) of trains crossing the Cordillera Cantabrica; it is charmingly dedicated 'in homage to the railway, from the mountaineers and skiers of the region'.

* * *

One is tempted to think – not unkindly or patronisingly, though Spaniards may take it so – that whenever Spain undertakes something that will invite comparison with other countries – the organising of an international event or a technological advance – it will be poorly judged. It is not that Spaniards are technically incompetent but that they are somehow temperamentally predisposed to allow things to go wrong. In Spain's 'international year', 1992, the Barcelona Olympics went resoundingly right – because it was organised by Catalans, said the Catalans – while the international exhibition, Expo '92, in Seville was less than an unqualified success. That was because it was in Andalusia, said the Catalans. But there was more to it than that. Expo seemed to provide an excellent example of how Spain copes, and fails to cope, with the demands of modern life and business in the last decade of the twentieth century.

First, the good news. Perhaps the greatest success associated with Expo was the high-speed, 'bullet' train (AVE) which cut the journey time between Seville and Madrid from six hours to less than three. This was just the sort of high-tech service which one might have thought that Spain was incapable of producing to run reliably and on time. My own experiences with those lovable local trains that stop every five minutes did not give me much confidence that Spain could run a rail service for the twenty-first century between two business

122

centres. But I was quite wrong: the AVE train is very comfortable, quiet, quick and punctual. On a journey from Malaga to Madrid we joined the high-speed track at Cordoba and covered the four hundred kilometres from there to Madrid in under two hours. In 1992 this rail service was hailed as a ridiculously expensive 'white elephant' – even the railway station in Seville had to be moved – and little more than an ego-trip for the Sevillan prime minister, Felipe Gonzalez. But it works, and Spain is justifiably proud of it.

The commissioner general of Expo, Manuel Olivencia, said that one of its principal objectives was 'to transform Seville and Andalusia into an economic centre for the whole area of the western Mediterranean basin'. Three years on, 'technological parks' had been established in Seville and Malaga, attracting companies such as Fujitsu and Siemens, and a consortium, Andalucia Aerospacial, had been set up to make parts for Boeing, Airbus and McDonnell Douglas in the region. Andalusia has one of the best motorway networks in Spain (in addition to the best train service); but it still remains largely non-industrial and, at a figure in excess of thirty per cent, has the highest rate of unemployment of any region in the European Union. Perhaps it should, and always will, stick to flamenco, bullfighting and tourism.

The high-tech, futuristic qualities of Expo certainly looked out of place in Seville when the universal exhibition opened on Easter Monday, 20 April 1992. During Holy Week Seville is a remarkable place to be, with hooded processions of penitents dripping their candle-grease on the streets after dark, and flamenco laments which, as their name (*saeta*) describes, arrow through the air of the city by day and night. Two weeks after Easter the *feria* begins, with its parades of horse-drawn carriages, girls with polka-dot flounces, and bullfights every day in the Maestranza ring. Between these two events – the one hallowed by the passion of Christ, the other by local, and national, tradition – Expo '92 was launched.

The idea had first been mooted by King Juan Carlos in the 1970s, to celebrate the five hundreth anniversary of the discovery of America by Columbus in 1492. (That was also the year in which the Moors and Jews were finally expelled from Spain.) For the next two centuries Seville, and Spain, enjoyed a golden age: Seville was the trade capital of the New World. Much of the wealth which the treasure ships carried up the 'river of gold', the Guadalquivir, to Seville was spent on grand houses, churches and public buildings. Several dukes – Feria, Alba, Medinaceli – built their palaces; and a magnificent Archive of the Indies was established, containing more than thirty thousand documents on the discoveries of the New World. But by the early eighteenth century Seville's bonanza was coming to an end and, as one *madrileño* put it to me, 'the city has been going downhill ever since'.

The attitude of Spaniards from Madrid and the north to Andalusians is not unlike the view taken by the English of the Irish in the nineteenth century. A delightful people, the *sevillanos*, but you couldn't leave them to run something like Expo; and so, to their great irritation, not to say humiliation, most of the senior posts in the Expo administration were filled by officials from Madrid and Barcelona. There were two things in Andalusia, however, that even the brightest outsiders were unable to do anything about: the weather, and the almost infinite capacity for greed and corrupt practices of those with both Latin and Arab blood coursing in their veins.

Little more than two years before Expo opened, Seville had a month of almost continuous rain. When I visited the five hundred-acre site, on the island of La Cartuja, between two branches of the Guadalquivir, it was not much more than a quagmire. An electronic sign announcing the number of days before 20 April 1992 – then about eight hundred and fifty – was hardly reassuring. By the time that day came round, Seville was enjoying its customary spring temperatures of around 30°C, and by early summer would be living up to its reputation as the oven of Spain. Valiant efforts were made to create a bio-climate on parts of the exhibition site, by spraying water in order to draw heat from the air. But one wonders how many people, foreigners in particular, were dissuaded from going to Expo by the knowledge that it was being held between April and October in probably the hottest place in Europe. By the end of its six months Expo had attracted only two thirds of the number of visitors expected.

Just as inevitable as the searing summer heat, and probably an equal deterrent to visitors, were the shenanigans resulting in absurdly high hotel prices. In spite of cautionary advice from the city council, Seville doubled its hotel prices as well as its hotel capacity; and the experience of one new hotel, named after the heir to the throne, Felipe, Principe de Asturias, was not untypical. Three striking circular towers on the edge of the exhibition site were standing empty at Easter 1992. The company that built them had gone into liquidation: investment monies were allegedly squandered and embezzled by members of the governing Socialist Workers' party (PSOE), and after construction workers had not been paid for several weeks they decided to sabotage the hotel's electrical and plumbing systems.

None of the big hotel operators wanted to take it on when they learned of the scale of 'commission payments' which were being demanded by various interests connected with the government. Eventually, however, an American group, Radisson, signed a management contract for up to five years and the hotel expanded its name to the grotesque-sounding Radisson Principe de Asturias Plaza. It finally opened a few weeks after Expo, charging around £340 per night for a double room and £1,375 for the 'royal' suite. Three years later it was charging £110 per night and calling itself the Principe de Asturias Radisson Hotel Sevilla.

Predictably, there were tales of corruption at every turn. Construction of the vast majority of pavilions was never put out to public tender, but arranged through the agency of the PSOE. Charges for services – electricity, water, food and drink –were extortionate and usually arranged through a government agency. It was virtually impossible to get tickets for the opera, because almost all of them had been taken by members of the junta (regional government) for their business associates, friends and relatives. The English travel agents which had secured allocations of opera tickets had them withdrawn.

It is Third World behaviour, one might think; while Spaniards would shrug their shoulders and ask what else you could expect from Andalusia and a corrupt Socialist government. It was hardly the way to run an exhibition at which almost every other country in the world was represented. And yet, in an extravagant and disordered way, Expo did establish Spain's place in the modern world. When plans were made to build Seville cathedral in the fifteenth century, the canons of the chapter resolved 'to erect such a huge temple that we shall go down to posterity as madmen'. History has not justified their predictions, though I did wonder, while visiting Expo, about the sanity of those responsible for building and organising the exhibition.

But the Andalusians loved it. Those who did not have to stay in hotels, and who didn't mind the heat, flocked to this fantastical vision of what the exhibition's promoters called 'the whole world on one island'. No doubt it amused them to see that the pavilions of Spain's autonomous regions, which had been sited next to the Latin American pavilion, housing Spain's former colonies, were now diplomatically separated by the United Nations.

However, the Andalusian visitors were not bringing business to the city: so many locals paid £170 for a six-month pass that the offer of a season ticket had to be suspended. But Seville did gain some tangible benefits from Expo, apart from a business park on the edge of the city (which is what Expo became after 1992, though many of its pavilions remained empty) and a lot of new hotels. The *ayuntamiento* (city hall) was successfully restored, and opened by the King, complete with ornamented facade and its magnificent double staircase, which was saved at the insistence of the Duke of Segorbe, who was unofficial adviser to the restoration.

The total cost of Expo was hard to quantify, though a figure of £6 billion, to include the high-speed train and the infrastructure of new roads and airport, was probably not too wide of the mark. Much of this was borrowed by the central government at high rates of interest on external credit markets. By the end of Expo in October 1992, harsh reality had returned: the peseta was devalued (three times in nine months) and inflation, interest rates and unemployment were on the rise. Meanwhile a lot of people connected with the PSOE had lined their pockets, thanks to Expo, and the major corruption scandals of the 1990s, involving government ministers and public officials, were still to come. While the opposition would blame it all on the Socialist party, which had held power for too long, and the press wondered whether corruption was a price which Spain had to pay for democracy, others recalled that there was really nothing very new under the Spanish sun. Political and commercial corruption were fairly common in Franco's day, though not, of course, reported; and in 1935 the prime minister, Alejandro Lerroux, was involved in a financial scandal with three gentlemen named Strauss, Perez and Lopez, which resulted in the word *estraperlo* passing into the language.

Nor, in spite of the legacy of Expo, have there been many real changes in Andalusia – except in the number of golf courses (fifty-three in 1995, out of a total of one hundred and forty-five in mainland Spain). Tourism and agriculture remain the principal industries; the people remain attached to the *pueblo* and the land. In summer they winnow the wheat, in December they pick the olives – and they still make marmalade with apricots rather than the bitter Seville oranges which were given them for the purpose. In the bars they still talk of the bulls, as well as football, and they still resolutely ignore 'No Smoking' signs.

NINE

Fishy Tales

The three-thousand-ton trawler *Sil* had docked the previous night beneath the bridge that straddles Vigo Bay. Its eighty-man crew had been fishing in the South Atlantic for the past five months, but the vessel was returning to its home port for the first time in three years. The fishing grounds, for the *Sil* and twenty other similar boats, almost all of which were Spanish, are off the Falkland Islands; they can catch up to seventy-five tons per day; and the name of this very lucrative game is squid.

To any British trawlerman, a few minutes on board the *Sil* would be something of a revelation. It is a floating freezer factory: the vast nets, having been hauled over the stern by enormous winches, empty their catch below deck, where the conveyor-belt operation begins. The squid are cleaned and cut by machines (which in the close season are adapted for cleaning, heading, tailing and filleting hake), then placed on trays which are laid on shelves for freezing, initially at −30°C, in the hold. Above the factory, accommodation for the crew is spacious, and the bridge is a mass of buttons and computer screens. By swivelling on his stool the skipper can simultaneously control both the winching gear and the course and speed of his boat.

Once the *Sil* has caught and stored its full capacity of squid (one thousand tons, which may take between two and four weeks), it makes for the Falklands, transfers its catch to a huge freezer platform in Port Stanley harbour and resumes fishing. A transport ship will bring the

frozen squid home to Vigo, where almost all of it is destined for the Spanish market.

A number of significant points arise here, all of them worth considering next time a 'fish war' is declared, whether between Spain and Britain or Spain and Canada or, almost inevitably, Spain and someone. Before we rush to condemn this indiscriminate predator of the seas, a few things need explaining.

Spaniards are passionate about fish, eating almost five times more, per head, than we do in Britain. If some stocks in European waters are low, there is no shortage of fish elsewhere, particularly in the southern hemisphere. Spanish fishermen, at any rate those who come from Galicia and the Basque country, are prepared to spend most of the year away from home. Spanish fishing technology and fishing-boat design are more advanced than in any other country in Europe, and in the world are equalled only by Japan and New Zealand. Spaniards are prepared to go almost literally to the ends of the earth to catch fish, and are not deterred by potentially hostile or precarious political environments.

The Falklands are a case in point. Spain supported Argentina's invasion of 'Las Malvinas' in 1982, but it was the first country after the war to make joint venture fishing agreements with the Foreign Office and the Falkland Islanders. Because of Argentina's continuing claim to the islands, the Spanish boats are not welcome in Buenos Aires – an enjoyable irony, since the largest number of Galician émigrés to Central and South America lives in Argentina. The boats have to go to Punta Arenas in Chile for major refits and their crews travel home via Montevideo. They don't talk about 'Las Malvinas' any more.

'I like doing business with the Falkland Islanders, because they are straightforward and reliable,' one owner told me. 'Unlike the Africans and Arabs – and Spanish – who demand backhanders.'

Spaniards are prepared to admit to corruption in their business and politics, but not to misbehaviour in the catching of fish. There was anger, and bewilderment, at the Canadian action against the Vigo-based *Estay* in the so-called halibut war in the North Atlantic in 1995. The confiscated catch was returned and legal action taken against the Canadian government for having arrested the Spanish boat in international waters, outside the two-hundred-mile limit. Far from taking 'Canada's halibut', Spaniards say that Canada has never caught this fish in deep water. The culprits who are really responsible for depleting the coastal fish stocks are Canadian seals.

You have only to spend a few hours in this city – Vigo is the largest fishing port, and the largest fishing-boat builder, in Europe – to begin to understand the significance of fishing and fish to the Galicians. Fresh and frozen fish landed in Galicia account for more than half the Spanish total; and the number of people in the region employed in fishing and related industries represents fifty per cent of the working population. Don Alfonso Paz-Andrade, chairman of Pescanova, which has a hundred and forty freezer fishing boats engaged in joint venture contracts around the world, told me:

> For us fishing is more than just a job; it's a bit like a vocation. Until quite recently Galicia had no proper roads; we have always considered that our road was the sea. Franco, himself a Galician, purposely kept the region backward, so we have lived and made money from the sea.
>
> When our crews come back to Vigo after fishing for five months off Namibia or Mozambique, they stay at home for a few weeks and then they come to me and say, 'Don Alfonso, I have pleased my wife and paid my debts; please send me back to sea where I belong.'

Perhaps British fishermen once thought like that, but not any more. After the cod war with Iceland, boats were laid up or sold and Britain appeared to lose interest in fish and fishing. There was an alternative – the long-distance, deep-water fishing developed by Spain – but there was not the capital or the commitment. Nor was there the passion for eating fish. One December Pescanova chartered an Antonov military transport aircraft, crewed by Russians, to fly a hundred tons of large prawns from Mozambique to Vigo to meet increased demand over Christmas.

It was Pescanova that pioneered the idea, in the 1960s, of freezer boats capable of spending more than two weeks at sea, and then embarked on joint ventures with foreign governments in the 1970s, when the United Nations recognised the right of coastal states to impose two-hundred-mile limits.

Paz-Andrade insists it is primarily an attitude of mind that enables Spain to operate these fisheries successfully; among Europeans, only Iberian fishermen (Spanish and Portuguese) are prepared to spend up to five months at a time away from home. What, then, of the charge that Spain takes too much fish, putting stocks at risk?

'This is a lot of nonsense,' Paz-Andrade said. 'If stocks of a particular

131

species are running low, it will become uneconomic for the boats to go on fishing for them, and so they will go elsewhere and catch something else until the fish stocks are renewed, which normally happens very quickly.

'The best way to conserve stocks is to be guided by prudent financial policy: take the annual interest but beware of touching the capital.'

He would like to play a part in establishing an international legal framework for fishing on the high seas, not only as a result of the *Estay* incident but because of the new sources of protein which Paz-Andrade believes are to be found at depths of around one thousand metres. Vast quantities of a fish called orange roughy are being caught off New Zealand, and Paz-Andrade believes they are also to be found in deep water in the North Atlantic, possibly off Scotland. If they are within the two-hundred-mile coastal limit, they may need to be regulated by the Common Fisheries Policy, for which Paz-Andrade reserves his special contempt.

'It is a policy of hypocrisy,' he said. 'There are conservation measures and all sorts of inspections, but only of licensed boats. The illegal boats, of which about seventy operate in European Community waters – from France, Spain, Holland and Britain – are never touched. They are not bothered about fishing with an illegal net-mesh size, because they are breaking the law by fishing at all.'

One might imagine that Spaniards would be quite happy with the Common Fisheries Policy, since it does not appear to work to their disadvantage. In fact, they consider its operation to be so inefficient that the regulations need to be completely rewritten, permitting fewer boats, with better policing and stricter controls on over-fishing. At the same time it is generally acknowledged that the 'social interest' of fishing communities operating small boats off the coasts of, say, the west of England and Ireland should be protected. The Common Fisheries Policy undoubtedly works against Britain, if only because the majority of European Community fishing grounds are in what would otherwise be exclusively British waters. The current share-out may be inequitable to Britain, but countries such as Spain do not have the advantage of a continental shelf.

Spaniards acknowledge, of course, that they have taken some of

Britain's quotas by buying British fishing boats or operating Spanish boats under British licences. But it is worth remembering that those boats are obliged to call at a British port four times every three months, paying harbour dues, and that they should pay tax in Britain on their catch, wherever it is sold.

The latest gripe from British fishermen was that forty foreign boats had been authorised to fish in the Irish Box from the beginning of 1996. When I put this to Paz-Andrade, he laughed. 'This is only a sentimental thing. We have an Irish company, Eiranova, which has five boats flying the Irish flag. They very seldom go into the Irish Box, because the fishing is better outside.'

Perhaps British fishermen might in future consider their position more objectively and the British press eschew the tired old clichéd comparison with the Spanish Armada. Spain is not responsible for the plight of our fishermen, nor is it any more responsible than France for breaking the rules, for instance on under-sized fish.

Talking of which, it was time to go and inspect Vigo's fish market. This is not something which the official EU inspectors do very often, according to a market trader, and when they appear they are usually 'friendly'. This presumably meant that they do not take their measuring tapes to the boxes of little fish lined up on the concrete floor of the market sheds, waiting to be auctioned at 7 am. One problem is to know whether they are immature fish which have barely started to grow or little, mature fish which have grown to their full size. The difficulty is compounded by the fact that they may have obscure and confusing regional names. A small hake is known here as *carioca* but in Andalusia as *pijota*, which elsewhere in Spain means a codling. As one trader said to me, 'If small fish are caught in the nets, why throw them back dead?'

A few hours earlier I had watched long-liners unloading swordfish, and trawlers their haul of sharks, together with baskets of offal, slippery and shining in the rain. Blood, too, glistened on the quay. Between 1 am and the start of the auction some four thousand people would be milling around, many of them women, known as *moscas* (flies), who work through the night in their green and yellow rubber gloves, sorting the fish according to size and species. There was

133

skate, squid, octopus, grouper, bream, conger eel, sole, turbot, cod and, of course, the Spaniards' favourite, hake.

By seven o'clock porters were pushing barrows, the sharks and swordfish were laid out at one end of the long shed, boxes of shellfish at the other, while a prospective buyer, wanting to inspect a box of hake, upturned it on to the floor. The fishy, noisy scene seemed unchanged since the last century. It was all very different from the freezer factory ships lying at anchor a few hundreds yards away.

Now some of the *moscas* became buyers, taking cash and calculators out of their apron pockets. There was a flurry of bidding for a box of barnacles, known as *percebes*, which are curious finger-like creatures about two inches long with a triangular black-and-white tip sometimes likened to an elephant's toenail. Their texture is rather rubbery, but they may cost up to £75 per kilo because collecting them is a rather hazardous operation.

Percebes grow on rocks buffeted by the Atlantic on the exposed parts of the Galician coast near Cape Finisterre. They are gathered by a man on the end of a rope who is lowered over the cliff-face by a companion. He must cut the barnacles quickly from the rock as the waves recede, then be hauled out of danger before the sea smashes against the rocks once more. This is known as the Costa de la Muerte (Death Coast): of the two hundred licensed barnacle-gatherers, about fifteen are killed every year. Here, surely, was final confirmation that, when it comes to harvesting the fruits of the sea, the Spanish are different.

In view of the dangers involved in their collection, the eating of *percebes* is considered to be *muy macho*: it is unquestionably a manly thing to do. More feminine in character are shellfish such as mussels, which are simply cultivated. One does not immediately associate Spain with mussels, but it is a fact that sixty-five per cent of the total European mussel market comes from these coasts; and ninety-five per cent of the mussels sold in Spain are grown in Vigo Bay. Near the northern shore, lines of floating platforms stretch seaward towards the Islas Cies which guard the entrance to the bay. At a distance these platforms rather resemble oriental houseboats; beneath them hundreds of thousands of mussels are grown on long ropes.

Elvers (*angulas*) come into the northern estuaries, having journeyed, as all eels apparently are wont to do, from the Sargasso Sea. But demand cannot be satisfied from Spanish rivers alone: elvers are also imported from Cornwall and from the Severn estuary. (The Japanese take English elvers and grow them on for two years before selling them.) One of the most important things to know about *angulas*, I was told by a Basque restaurant owner, is how to kill them. They should be wrapped in a tobacco leaf in order to bring out their flavour. Northern Spaniards are now extending their fish menus even further by marketing lampreys, those curious little eel-like suckers that attach themselves to stones. They should be aware that King Henry I was said to have died of a surfeit of them.

Tuna have provided the principal *casus belli* between Britain and Spain – more specifically, between Cornish and Basque fishermen – over the past few years. The fishery takes place during the summer months in the Bay of Biscay. Spanish boats outnumber British by about fifteen to one, but it is the British boats that fish for tuna using huge catch-all (including dolphins) drift nets up to two and a half kilometres long, while the Spanish boats use baited long-lines. Spain would seem to have the best of the argument here about which method is the more ecologically sound. Drift-netted tuna are likely to be bruised and damaged, and they will be sold for processing; while tuna caught on a line will be sold fresh and command a higher price.

The Spanish method involves fixed poles trailing lines with false bait; while some boats use hand-held rods and live bait. Comparatively few tuna are landed in Galician ports; it is the Basques who have a virtual monopoly of these fish, whether following the yellow- and blue-fin tuna in the southern hemisphere, or the albacore (bonito) in the Bay of Biscay. Spain's major tuna ports are Burela and Bermeo, on the north coast, where around fifty per cent of the catch is landed.

Most of the Cornish tuna boats work out of Newlyn, at the far end of the county next to Penzance. Months after the *Estay* incident in the North Atlantic, Canadian flags were still flying all over Newlyn. It was not only the boats tied up in harbour and the fish merchants, but also the newsagent, the chemist and the local car dealer – all were sporting the red maple leaf. 'Support Cornish and Canadian fishermen' read one banner; it did not go on to say, 'against the common enemy, Spain', but the unwritten message was clear. So it is somewhat ironic that Cornish fishermen continue to sell a large proportion of their catch to Spain; and that on the road between Newlyn and Penzance the blue and gold logo of European unity is prominently displayed. (Penzance was burned by Spanish invaders in 1595, which may help to explain the continuation of hostilities four hundred years on.)

Pilchards, once the backbone of Cornwall's fishing industry, must be one of the very few fish that Spaniards can do without. Newlyn boasts Britain's last salt pilchard factory , but sells its output to northern Italy. The trade goes back to the last century, but may not last much longer. In the summer of 1995 I was told that the last pilchard catch had been off Plymouth the previous winter and that the only Newlyn man with the right gear for pilchard fishing had switched to beam trawling and was reluctant to lend his nets to anyone else.

Spaniards prefer their fish fresh, and such is the distribution network in Spain that, however far from the coast you may be, fresh fish can practically be guaranteed. Madrid may be in the middle of the country, but the overnight lorries will arrive before dawn each morning, from every major fishing port in Spain, laden with all manner of white fish and shellfish covered in crushed ice. In any fish market it is instructive to watch shoppers inspecting before buying: they will look at the fish's eyes, and the condition of the skin, before comparing them with a neighbouring stall. The English housewife, on the other hand, would rather buy a piece of filleted plaice or haddock – or anything so long as its head, tail, innards and bones have been removed. Spanish cooks prefer to buy their fish whole and do all the preparation themselves. Producers of frozen fish products have found that the demand for whole octopus is much greater than for the pieces sliced and ready for the pan. Similarly, frozen scallops are more popular in the shell than on their own. As far as possible, the Spanish housewife wants to buy her fish looking as it did when it came out of the sea.

When it comes to *merluza* (hake), which could be classified as Spain's national fish, everything goes. You can buy packets of frozen hake steaks, hake centre cuts, hake tail pieces, hake fillets with skin, hake

fillets without skin. Hake are caught in European waters in Spanish boats; they are bought from other European markets and sold in Spain; they are caught off Namibia and sent home frozen; they are caught off Chile and flown home fresh. When it gets to the kitchen, hake should be cooked, according to my own experience, *a la gallega* – simply baked or grilled, with a sauce of olive oil, crushed garlic and sweet paprika, which should be poured over the fish and a few boiled potatoes. Especially in northern Spain, *kokotxas* (hake chins) is a popular dish.

While fish is always available, and is usually the best thing to choose, in restaurants all over Spain, it is the northern Spaniards – Galicians, Basques, Catalans – who claim the most 'serious' attitudes to gastronomy. Of the restaurants awarded rosettes in the Spanish Michelin guide, the vast majority are north of Madrid, and only three are in Andalusia. Arzak, in San Sebastian, is often described as the best restaurant in Spain. Though I have not paid that sort of price (£50 per head) for a meal in Spain, the more adventurous cooking which I have sampled both in San Sebastian and in Barcelona has not always been successful. Once Spaniards try to be imaginative in the kitchen, things can start to go wrong. I recall a *besugo* (sea-bream) in Oviedo, stuffed with squid, prawns, peppers and mushrooms in a green olive sauce, which plainly did not work. More memorably, I once had a delicious all-salmon lunch in a restaurant in a small provincial Galician town: a sort of gravadlax, heavily olive-oiled, followed by salmon marinated raw in fresh lime juice and chopped with capers and hard-boiled egg, followed by an escalope of salmon lightly grilled with a sorrel sauce.

In the south one is better off sticking to plainly grilled or fried fish – it is the Andalusians, according to other Spaniards, who are responsible for eating little fish – and the wealth of shellfish, which can often be eaten more cheaply, by the *racion* or *media racion*, in *tapas* bars. What a fine meal one can make, at the bar, of a few dishes of *mejillones* (mussels), *almejas* (clams), *boquerones* (fresh anchovies soused in garlic), *chipirones* (little squid), a *salpicon de mariscos* (prawns and crab in a spicy sauce) and plenty of fresh bread.

TEN

Of Babies, Bonfires and Bestas

One way to observe the unchanged face of Spain, in a bizarre and extreme form, is by visiting the village *fiestas* which are held, in one place or another, during every month of the year. There are pagan rites, reminders of the Inquisition, weird celebrations in honour of various saints, and quite a bit of cruelty to animals. I have occasionally thought of spending a year attending these *fiestas* – with a precise timetable and a fast car it would be possible to take in five or six a month – but one would be in danger of coming away with a warped view of Spain. However intriguing are the country's traditions and religious history, one would probably not want to witness more than one bull-baiting, Judas burning or ritual battle between Moors and Christians – guess who wins!

But there are plenty of other strange goings-on in remote villages during the year. In January, at Guarrate in Zamora, cockerels are hung by their feet in the village square so that men on horses can try to decapitate them with swords. A similar event takes place at La Alberca, Salamanca, in April, when young men, having drunk large quantities of red wine, attempt to snap a suspended cockerel's head off with their hands as they ride past. They do the same thing with geese in El Carpio de Tajo, Toledo, during July. The men who do their best, while blindfolded, to club well-fattened cockerels to death in November at Salas de los Infantes, Burgos, are paying homage to Santa Cecilia.

The bull-baiting *fiestas* and *encierros* (where bulls are run through the streets) are often held in honour of saints. By a typically Spanish irony, St Francis of Assisi, who looked upon all animals as his brothers and sisters, is honoured at several bull *fiestas* during October. Such celebrations may involve *toros de fuego*, where flares are attached to their horns after dark. At Tordesillas, Valladolid, a bull is chased across a bridge over the Douro river and speared with lances. The person responsible for killing the beast is awarded its testicles, which he carries home on the point of his lance.

I have seen a promotional leaflet describing the attractions of the annual *fiestas* in three languages – Spanish, French and English – which refers to 'the killing of animals' (in Spanish and French) but, in the English translation, to 'carnival celebrations'. It is hardly surprising that some of the *fiestas* attract unwelcome publicity in Britain. At Coria, Caceres, in Estremadura, Midsummer Day is celebrated each year by letting loose a bull in the square so that the locals can throw firecrackers and darts at it. After some time the bull is dispatched with a shotgun. In view of the bad press which the *fiesta* has received, foreigners are told they will have to face the bull if they try taking photographs. In 1995 an English animal rights campaigner, Vicki Moore, got so close to the bull with her camera that the threat was unnecessary: she was badly gored and spent several weeks in hospital. When she returned home she said she was sorry the bull was killed.

At other village festivals, witches are burnt in effigy in Llanes, Asturias; the women of Vinuesa, Soria, beat the men of the village with pine branches; and in Santoña, Santander, they dance round a pine tree singing its praises – for being so straight and erect. A transvestite known as Madre Cochina runs though the streets of San Pablo de los Montes, Toledo, attended by two acolytes dressed as cows who lift women's skirts; in La Puebla del Caraminal, on the Atlantic coast near Santiago de Compostela, parents carry their children in open caskets to ward off the threat of death; and in Castrillo de Murcia, Burgos, a clown figure leaps over babies lying on mattresses in the streets, thereby inoculating them against disease and the devil.

West of the city of Burgos, on the plains of Old Castile, people converge on the village of Castrillo de Murcia, on the Sunday after

Corpus Christi, for one of the strangest *fiestas* in the calendar. It is partly pagan, partly religious, in both parts dominated by a masked and costumed burlesque figure known as El Colacho, who wears yellow and red and brandishes a horse-hair whip. When I arrived in the square below the church, eight members of the local *cofradía* (guild) were gathered by the fountain, wearing dark suits, caped cloaks and homburg hats. Their leader had on a black top hat and tail-coat, and was carrying a very large green drum. They might have been burgomasters from Bavaria rather than burghers of the province of Burgos.

As they processed at a stately pace through the narrow village streets, to the insistent beating of the drum, they were joined by El Colacho (wearing trainers), who ran ahead and then back to the drum. As far as I could understand it, at this stage of the proceedings El Colacho represents a devil-figure; laying about him with his wooden-handled whip, he chases the youngsters who hurl insults at him as they run past. This is known as the *corrida* (running), though it seemed more like an *encierro* (where, as in Pamplona, the bulls are run through the streets). El Colacho appeared as the bull, pursuing the young lads as they taunted him, but kept under at least partial control by the accompanying burghers, who were playing the role of the steers. I was reminded of Pamplona several times by the frightened cries of boys flattening themselves against street doors and walls.

When the procession returned to the square it dispersed, and we climbed the steps to the church to celebrate Mass. Above the south door Santiago was slaying his enemies from a horse which had lost its stone head. Even more than in other villages, this church dominates Castrillo from its eminence at the top of the hill; and all the narrow streets seem to lead up to it. During Mass there was standing room only and we sang a hymn to the tune of the Simon and Garfunkel song, *Sounds of Silence*. Sung by a congregation of hundreds, it was very affecting; indeed the happy, festive atmosphere was such that, when we came to the 'sign of peace', for the first time I did not feel embarrassed to turn and shake my neighbour's hand.

After the service another *corrida* took place round the streets, ending in the square when El Colacho and his burgher steers disappeared through an arch and into the darkness of what appeared to be the village hall. A large crowd was now gathering in the square when, two minutes later, women began to emerge from the hall, bearing tray after tray of *orejuelas*, triangular-shaped sponge biscuits, and followed by more local helpers carrying jugs of red wine and plastic cups. I think the wine was diluted, but so what? We were the guests of the village, enjoying an unheralded lunchtime cocktail party in the sun.

As the party was breaking up, a flock of sheep appeared at one corner of the square, before being driven uphill towards some pasture. There was a powerful smell of horse manure, and a cock crew. The men of the *cofradia*, still in their cloaks and now carrying wooden staffs with gilded tops, went off to their homes. One was carrying a basket which contained some money and two eggs. It was the time of the *siesta*, before the next procession at five o'clock. Then El Colacho was accompanied by male dancers, in white collarless shirts with red and green crossed braces, brown breeches and white stockings. They wore blue cummerbunds and blue or red headbands. Fewer boys now followed El Colacho, and he had little use for his horse-hair whip. When they got back to the square below the church, it was time for vespers.

For the first few minutes of the service, the drummer, without his top hat, marched up and down the aisle giving single beats on his great drum which, within the confines of this cavernous building, made a fearsome sound. Behind him walked the priests, from the altar to the west door, where he turned and led El Colacho, now unmasked, up the aisle to the altar, then back to the west door again. The final procession, from west door to altar, was led by El Colacho, followed by the drummer and the priests swinging incense. Clearly the comic devil-figure had been banished; it seemed, in view of the tricks he was about to perform after the service, that he had now been translated into a sort of shaman. Vespers then proceeded conventionally, but towards the end the drum was suddenly banged again with such force that the woman beside me jumped and started to shake. Thoughts of the Inquisition briefly crossed my mind. Then we all made our way out of church and down the steps to the square. Banners were unfurled, and little girls in white bridesmaids' dresses carried baskets of red rose petals. There before us was the most amazing sight: babies were being laid out on mattresses on the ground. Four to a mattress, they lay happily enough on pillows, in romper suits or nightdresses, shaking their white-socked feet in the evening sun.

The babies' mothers knelt by the mattresses, offering words of encouragement, then backed away as El Colacho approached, still carrying his horse-hair whip though now, with his face unmasked, the picture of benevolence. As he walked past one mattress, the crowd stepped back to give him room. After a few yards he turned, started his run-up and jumped cleanly over the length of the mattress and the

143

four bemused babies still lying there and showing no concern as a pair of tennis shoes flashed over their heads. Then a second Colacho appeared – I'm not sure from where – and performed the same routine. He was followed by a procession of priests, walking beneath a golden canopy held by six strong men, who blessed the babies and swung incense over their heads. As they moved on, the little girls in long white dresses, some of them accompanied by boys dressed in military uniform, threw their rose petals over the babies' heads.

This ceremony was repeated several times as the procession continued round the village. More babies, all supposedly born in the previous twelve months, were laid out in the street, and after the Colachos had successfully completed their long-jumping over two mattresses which each contained six babies, a prayer was said through a portable microphone that looked more like a cellnet telephone. The blessing was given, then '*silencio para los niños*' was called, and the crowd moved on, almost seeming to engulf the innocent babes, who were hurriedly snatched up by their mothers and taken home. By now it was almost seven o'clock; even for a Spanish baby, it was time for milk and bed.

I asked one woman, who might have been on the mattress herself some sixty summers ago, what all these delightful goings-on actually signified. El Colacho had been defeated, she said; the forces of good had triumphed over evil and – as far as I could understand her – the jumping over the babies represented the flight of the devil. By this act they were now protected against any evil or harmful influences and, since the *fiesta* is associated with the festival of Corpus Christi, they received benediction in honour of the Eucharist.

Led by flags and a large cross which rose above the multitude, the procession passed balconies draped with sheets and lace cloth, Some doorways had been converted into little altars, hung with white sheets bearing images of the Virgin and decorated with roses, geraniums and cushions. As we turned a corner, a car radio was noisily commentating on a bicycle race, and a street stall offered ice creams, *churros* and olives. The procession made its way uphill to the church for the last time, where prayers were said and a final drumbeat was heard. An elderly couple were looking forward to a recital of Castilian music later that evening in the square, accompanied by *pan, queso y vino*. But I was headed west, across the cornfields and down the straight road to Sahagun.

That bulls and chickens suffer at the hands of villagers in various *fiestas* across Spain can hardly be denied; and most would agree that the cruelty is gratuitous. But it would be quite wrong to conclude that Spaniards are temperamentally cruel to all animals: they are just as soppy about dogs as the British. They may adopt a different attitude to some animals from that which we would take. It is sometimes a question of having less respect for the 'feelings' of animals – a subject for debate elsewhere – while according more respect to humankind. Such thoughts were passing through my head when witnessing the *fiesta* known as *A Rapa das Bestas* in the village of Sabucedo, in the province of Pontevedra, Galicia.

Wild horses, which live all the time in the hills, are rounded up once a year, at the end of June, and around a hundred and fifty at a time are herded into an enclosure on the edge of the village. It is a little like a small, square bullring, with stone tiered seats. The purpose of this exercise is twofold: to brand the foals and clip the manes and tails of the horses to rid them of lice, and to give the lads of the *pueblo* the opportunity to show their bravery and strength as they wrestle the animals to the ground.

Bagpipes were playing on the terraces as we climbed, in pouring rain, up stone steps to the top of the enclosure. 'Respect the animals' announced the programme which I had been handed. It also said that the *encierro* at Pamplona was child's play compared with this. The horses, most of them brown with black manes, came down the street, twelve or twenty at a time, and, to much shouting and stick-waving, through a corrugated iron gateway and into the enclosed area below us. After fifteen minutes it was filled with a mass of wet horse-flesh, overseen by an old man with only one arm, which held a knobbled stick. The horses appeared remarkably docile, until the gate was closed and a dozen or more young men began to wade through them, grabbing foals wherever they could. Once a foal had been restrained, it was manhandled, not always gently, outside to a small high-walled stone yard where they would later be branded. As the horses began to get unsettled, moving in waves against each other, steam started to rise from their flanks drenched by sweat and the persistent warm rain.

It got worse when the young toughs started on the horses. Some of them leaped down from the stone seats, like *espontaneos* into the bullring, straight on to the horses' backs, which they then proceeded to ride rodeo-style until the animals could be dragged to the ground, to cheers and applause from the spectators. It takes three or four men to bring a horse down, then two to hold its head, while another grabs the tail and swiftly clips it before doing the same job on the mane. The horse gets to its feet apparently none the worse for the experience, and another animal is approached for the same treatment. The rain eased for a while, before a thunderstorm broke over this curious scene of wet, writhing bodies – wild horses and wild men together.

Undoubtedly the RSPCA would have disapproved. Most of the horses would have been very distressed; there were mares in foal, as well as mares which had temporarily had their foals removed from them, and stallions that reared up on their hind legs and sparred with each other. To my eyes it was not an attractive sight, and it appeared to be cruel.

But there is probably no other practical way of clipping the manes and tails of wild horses and ridding them of lice and other parasites which infest them as they roam in these hills. There are smaller round-ups in other hill villages, but Sabucedo is the big one, the one which is described as being of 'national tourist interest'. Ironically, because of its size, the press of well over a hundred horses in such an enclosed space and the over-enthusiasm of some of those taking part, it is also the one to which tourists are most likely to take exception.

To the Spaniard, the *rapa* does not connote any lack of respect for the horses and, which is equally or more important, it gives young men the opportunity to gain respect among their fellows and their girlfriends. Needless to say, there is also a religious aspect to this *fiesta*, which is held in homage to San Lorenzo. In the sixteenth century two such horses were supposedly offered to the saint to persuade him to rid the country of plague. Today the tradition persists with the nicking of the ears of a few chosen horses which are dedicated to San Lorenzo – though someone told me that a wild horse with a damaged ear was as

likely to have been attacked by a wolf in the hills as to have been singled out for special treatment in honour of the saint.

As the rain continued the horse-play became more difficult – men and horses slipped and fell on the sodden ground – and, to everyone's relief, the activities were abandoned for the day. Dripping wet, we made our way to a bar in the village street and were soon restored by a glass of red wine and the traditional boiled octopus eaten from wooden bowls.

Midsummer provides the occasion for serious celebration in Spain. There are bull *fiestas*, such as the controversial one at Coria in

Estremadura, and on the night of 23 June (Midsummer's Eve) bonfires are lit for *la noche de San Juan*. At San Pedro de Manrique, Soria, the young men of the village, fortified through the evening by a sweet wine known as *zurracapote*, hoist girls on their shoulders as the fire dies down, and walk over the burning embers.

As much as anything, the welcoming of midsummer is an ancient Celtic ritual. However, the *Sanjuanes* that I attended one 23 June in the Basque country turned out to be something more. I was staying in San Sebastian and was directed to the *fiesta* at Hernani a few miles inland, an essentially modern town that had been badly damaged in the civil war. Market stalls on the edge of town, some of them run by Moroccans selling trinkets and leather, led uphill past flags and carnival bunting towards the main square, Plaza Berri. I got there in the early evening of a stiflingly hot day (37° according to the electronic indicator) to find families wandering about, bands playing, children eating ice-creams and carrying coloured balloons. A cluster of Mickey Mouse balloons nodded their heads on the red, white and green bunting which was strung across the square. The atmosphere seemed happy, carefree, well suited to midsummer. Then I looked again at the flags.

On every white one was written the word '*Amnistia*'; the red and green flags bore a sinister black logo, or the outline of men's faces. So this was an ETA stronghold; the feeling of *fiesta* suddenly seemed to go very flat. (I learnt afterwards that the three towns of Hernani, Placencia and Villabona, all in the same part of Guipuzcoa, form what is known as the Death Triangle the most notorious breeding-ground for ETA.) Graffiti proclaiming '*Euskadira!*' and '*Amnistia Aldeko*' were daubed on walls round the square. '*Arrepentimiento o Muerte*' ('Repent or Die') was one of the more chilling messages on a wall above a bar, alongside a poster announcing a '*Marcha de Solidaridad*'. On one side of the square a little group of Basques in berets and white shirts sang songs for independence, while in another corner were posters promoting bisexuality and other sexual freedoms. It was a bizarre scene: surrounded by incitements to violence and perversion, children were climbing trees in the middle of the square and eating candy floss, while their mothers chatted at café tables or bargained for bolts of cloth stacked on trestle tables under the trees.

A few clarinettists and saxophonists joined the band of brass and drums that had been playing in the square. They began to make their way up a narrow street towards the *plaza* facing the church, where a bonfire was being prepared. Outside the church where Mass was being celebrated, a beggar woman was squatting with her child, but she moved away when the congregation came out. It was now around 8.30 pm, the heat was no less intense, and the bonfire remained unlit.

The area immediately outside the church door, and the balustraded steps, were being made ready for some midsummer pageant. Straw bales were being laid out, also bracken, earthenware pots and what looked like horse hair. There were girls draped in coloured scarves, with tattered aprons and carrying three-pronged sticks painted red. From beneath the arches of the town hall emerged grotesque figures on stilts, wearing sackcloth and with their faces hidden. Some had asses' heads, others black cloth masks and hoods hung with coloured, matted rope. I thought at one moment of Bottom in *A Midsummer Night's Dream*, and at another that these masked figures must be concealing ETA terrorists. They stalked around the square waving their arms in menacing fashion.

Behind the church the faces of ETA terrorists, printed on cloth posters, hung malevolently over the darkening, airless street. I hurried on to the intersection, where the setting sun projected its last shafts of horizontal light. More men and bands were advancing up the street towards the bonfire, which would soon be lit. But I was not inclined to stay until it got dark; there was an air about the place which was frightening, and I doubt if there was another foreigner, or indeed many Spaniards who were not Basque, in the centre of Hernani that night.

I got to my car on the outskirts of town as the Moroccans were packing up their stalls, and drove back to San Sebastian. Towards midnight I watched a bonfire burning on Mount Igueldo, overlooking La Concha Bay. Most of those surrounding it had come from a nearby restaurant, while some children made a smaller fire which they used for jumping practice. *El Diario Vasco* reported next day that there had been some dispute over the official flag to be used for the *fiesta* at Hernani. But, the article went on as if the unexpected had happened, the celebrations passed off peacefully.

ELEVEN

Terrorists of the North

Among the friends of King Alfonso XIII and Queen Ena, there was much toing and froing every summer between San Sebastian and Biarritz, during the years after their marriage in 1906. The king and queen, who had done much of their courting in these two rather similar resorts, continued for some years to drive over to Biarritz for polo and tea parties. On their countless journeys, which took them across the frontier at Irun, it is doubtful whether they gave even a passing glance, five miles out of San Sebastian, to what was then no more than the village of Renteria, close to the port of Pasajes.

Half a century later, Renteria was to be the beneficiary of one of the housing programmes initiated by the Franco government. They served a social need at the time: the industrial revolution was under way and Franco, the paternalist dictator, would provide. But he did not know what he would be providing: featureless blocks of low-cost housing, built without planning on the fringes of Spanish cities, became the seed-beds of crime and vice. The story differs only in degree from what was happening elsewhere in Europe, not least in Britain, during the 1960s. In some places, of course, the standards of construction, the corrupt profiteering, the lack of planning were worse than in others; but there can be few grimmer legacies of this time than Renteria. Lured by the prospect of jobs in the industrialised Basque country, migrants came from Castile and Leon and Renteria's

population more than doubled in twenty years. The aspect of the town today is such that one might think it had been blighted by an earlier industrialised age. It is a place of unremitting urban gloom, where it is hard to escape the stench of sewage from the river. It was little wonder that Renteria, by 1982 a town of some forty-six thousand inhabitants, had more than its share of urban crime – drugs, street gangs, homosexual prostitution, murder. But there was more to Renteria than that: overcrowding, poverty and dereliction brought a

151

new criminal element to this benighted town. It became a notorious breeding-ground for ETA terrorists.

One of them was Idoia Lopez, born in 1964, the daughter of parents who had migrated to the north coast from Salamanca. However, ETA had been born five years earlier, before the *urbanizacion* of Renteria really got going. Euskadi Ta Askatasuna (Basque Homeland and Liberty) was the name given to the organisation formed in 1959 with the aim of establishing a democratic, independent Basque state. The armed struggle did not begin at once: ETA's original ideology closely followed the tenets of the Basque Nationalist party founded in 1894 with a reactionary programme – the work of its founding father, Sabino de Arana – which demanded not only the restoration of Basque independence but a return to its rural roots and a state based on families of exclusively Basque race. 'Seven provinces, one nation' was the slogan, embracing three districts of France (Soule, Labourd and Basse-Navarre) and four in Spain (Biscay, Guipuzcoa, Alava and Navarre).

The origins of the Basque people are, to say the least, unclear. It has been suggested that they are descended from Berber tribes, that they belong to a lost Atlantic continent, that their language is related to Georgian and to Magyar. What does seem more likely is that the Basques are an indigenous race, perhaps the last one in Europe, which kept itself apart from the other peoples of European history, never admitting outsiders and never moving beyond its Pyrenean homeland.

For most of its history the Basque country has been self-governing, in recent centuries subject to Spain's absolute monarchy. The ancient rights which Basques had acquired gave them privileges and safeguards (*fueros*) which each king would swear to observe. The provinces were recognised as *una tierra apartada* (a land apart), and it was not until 1876 that they were finally assimilated into the rest of Spain. The *fueros* were abolished ostensibly to punish those Basques who had supported Carlism; within a few years the nationalist party was founded and industrialisation began to change the character of the country and its people.

Though the kingdom of Navarre was the first independent Basque state, it is not strictly regarded as a Basque province, to the same extent as the other three – Guipuzcoa, Biscay and Alava. When the four historic provinces were offered autonomy by the republican government in 1932, it was rejected by Navarre, much of which was still a rigorously Catholic and Carlist stronghold and would support Franco in 1936. The other three provinces set up a provisional government of Euskadi after the outbreak of war; it was sworn in under the famous oak tree in the town of Guernica, recognised by all Basques as the sacred home of their liberties. Just over six months later, Guernica was destroyed by aircraft of the German Condor Legion. (In spite of the appalling devastation and loss of life, the parliament building, the oak tree and the church all survived.) After the war the Basques lost their *fueros*, their language and flag, and their repression by Franco was particularly severe.

It was worse for Basques than for the Catalans, who had a more secure cultural base. In Catalonia they had their artistic and architectural heritage – not to mention their economic and industrial wealth – their regional language was far more widely spoken and Catalan nationalism enjoyed more middle-class support. The Basques were less well able to cope with the years of isolation; the leaders of their nationalist party were getting old and feeble; the cause needed to reassert itself. The university students and young professional people who started ETA provided that opportunity.

The first violent deaths did not occur until 1968. The police reacted brutally and indiscriminately, and played into the terrorists' hands. Because of police methods, ETA attracted wide support across the region, often from non-Basques who found themselves arrested and suspected of involvement with ETA. By this time the ETA leadership had dropped its initial adherence to Arana's racist dogma, which would have excluded all those not of pure Basque origin. The immigrants from central Spain began to identify not only with the aspirations but also the methods of the people whose land they had come to share.

Franco did not know how to handle ETA, the new enemy whose active members probably never numbered more than a thousand. Much as he would have liked to, he couldn't carpet-bomb them, nor could he send a battalion of Moroccan troops to put them down, as he had done with ruthless success in Asturias in 1934. By this time, too, he was suffering the worsening effects of Parkinson's disease, and his judgment was becoming impaired. When sixteen Basques, including two priests, were tried by a military court in Burgos at the end of 1970, for the killing of a police officer, and six were sentenced to death, great pressure was brought on the *caudillo* – from within and outside his government – to reprieve the condemned men. Very reluctantly, he finally agreed to commute the sentences to thirty years' imprisonment, convincing himself that his decision confirmed the strength of his position and the success of his strategy against ETA. Two months before his death, however, Franco allowed five death sentences handed down by the Burgos court to be carried out. In spite of pleas, protests and recalled ambassadors, two members of ETA, and three of a Maoist organisation, were shot. Between these two Burgos trials, Franco's prime minister, Admiral Carrero Blanco, who had recently succeeded the *caudillo* as head of government, was assassinated in Madrid just before Christmas 1973. In an enormous explosion, his car was blown over a church, in what was the first major operation by ETA outside the Basque country.

Of course the ETA leadership realised it would lose support if the killing continued while Spain was getting ready for parliamentary democracy. But the lull in violence did not continue for long after the 1977 general elections. By now ETA was operating a network of small cells along classic terrorist guerrilla lines, and much of its training was taking place in Algeria and Libya. At the same time ETA recruits were infiltrating anti-terrorist police training courses in Spain. More than two hundred and fifty people were killed by ETA during the years 1978–80. In Renteria, as elsewhere in the Basque country, there was economic recession; factories were idle and more unemployed young were turning to violence. Idoia Lopez had passed her fifteenth birthday, and was ripe for recruitment.

By now ETA had split into two groups: ETA-*politico-militar*, which wanted to continue the proletarian struggle without resorting to violence, and ETA-*militar*, for whom the armed struggle was the only way to independence. ETA-*pm* was prepared to discuss less than complete independence for the Basque country. Once autonomy had been agreed, by statute in 1979, its goals were effectively achieved and its political wing, Euskadiko Ezkerra, merged with the Basque socialists.

But ETA-*militar* fought on for an 'independent socialist [i.e. Marxist-Leninist] state', incorporating Navarre as well as the other three Basque provinces. According to Herri Batasuna, ETA's own political party, Navarre was the 'mother of Euskadi', its heart and soul and spirit, and must be part of the Basque state even if, as was well-known to everyone, its inhabitants preferred to stay with Spain. The right of self-determination was apparently to be denied to the Navarrans. After autonomy was established, the Basque coat of arms included the emblem of Navarre as well as those of Guipuzcoa, Biscay and Alava. Following an application to court, however, the Navarran emblem was removed. But it can be seen on the coat of arms of Spain.

Herri Batasuna took part in elections but did not send its successful candidates to the parliaments of Guernica or Madrid. The aim, one of its leaders said, was to provoke a military occupation of the Basque country which would focus the struggle as between the Basques, led by ETA, and the Spanish oppressors. While the terrorists went on killing policemen in the north, they also targeted senior army officers in Madrid, murdering the military governor there and a general at the defence ministry. When the campaign was extended against Basques, especially Navarrans, opposed to ETA, and against tourists on Mediterranean beaches, the organisation began to lose support. However, the behaviour of the Guardia Civil towards their Basque, and not necessarily ETA, prisoners – clear evidence of torture and deaths in custody were not uncommon – was scarcely calculated to win sympathy for the forces of law and order. A police charge through the mean streets of Renteria did result in the dismissal of the police chief who had ordered it; but the cycle of terrorist violence, followed by brutal repression, followed by more violence, continued.

Special anti-terrorist squads were established, numbering six hundred men and drawn from the Guardia Civil and the Policia Armada; and at one time the number of policemen in the Basque country came to several thousand. Inevitably, their mistakes received wide publicity: announcements of the arrest, on the main road between Madrid and Bilbao, of the killers of Madrid's military governor, had to be followed by the embarrassed admission that the suspects in fact comprised the members of a pop group.

If there was an impressively large police presence in the Basque country at the end of the 1970s, it was not enough to satisfy senior officers in the armed forces. They thought the prime minister, Adolfo Suarez, and his interior minister, Rodolfo Martin Villa, were being soft on terrorism; and they thought no better of a fellow general, Gutierrez Mellado, who was defence minister. 'Spain yes! Democracy no!' was the cry of many army officers as they burnt Basque flags at the funeral of a murdered general.

Suarez was treading a difficult path between the fight against ETA and the grant of autonomy to the Basque country. The 1978 Constitution had recognised and guaranteed the right to autonomy of all regions of Spain; the Catalans and Basques had already petitioned the Cortes, and their statutes could not reasonably be delayed. Suarez did refuse and modify some of the Basque demands before agreeing their autonomy statute, but it satisfied the overwhelming majority of Basques – including ETA-*politico-militar*.

To the army this represented capitulation to the terrorists, in spite of all that the police were trying to do to suppress ETA-*militar* and contain the violence. The trouble was that, while the police might be good at carrying out arrests and indulging in old-fashioned interrogation techniques, they did not know how to tackle a highly disciplined guerrilla organisation. Nor did Suarez really understand the problem: he did not even visit the Basque country until the end of 1980, just before his resignation.

If ETA and Herri Batasuna really were hoping for military intervention, to undermine the democratic government and boost their cause, they nearly achieved it. Undoubtedly the attempted military coup of 23 February 1981 (see page 64 *et seq.*) was inspired, to a significant degree, by the frustration felt by the army at what it saw as the inability of a democratic civilian government to combat terrorism. ETA activity reached its peak in 1980, with ninety-two killings, and a fortnight before the Cortes was invaded by Colonel Tejero and his Guardia Civil, many officers were outraged when King Juan Carlos was heckled by members of Herri Batasuna when he bravely went to the Basque country to address the regional parliament.

Around this time forty per cent of unemployed Basques were said to support Herri Batasuna. It was not because Herri Batasuna had a policy for getting them work – it had no employment policy at all. Its appeal was that of an organisation fighting, literally, for the independence that at least held the hope of a better life than they were presently enduring. Soon after the Socialist Workers' party (PSOE), led by Felipe Gonzalez, won the 1982 general election, one of ETA's leaders was asked in an interview whether, in the light of all the recent changes in Spain, the time had come to moderate its policy. 'It won't change things as far as we are concerned,' he replied. 'We are not, nor have we been, nor shall we ever be Spaniards.'

Basque nationalists are a people of absolutes; they have never known liberalism. But there are two ironies here: first, that the vast majority of Basques have accepted Spanish national sovereignty; and secondly, that a number of ETA activists are not Basques by birth, but by adoption. In the early days of Basque nationalism they would not have qualified to represent the homeland.

The number of killings declined for a period in the 1980s: ETA suffered a lot of casualties and some of its original adherents no longer wished to be part of a group which in their opinion was now indistinguishable from a bunch of gangsters. At about this time, in 1984, Idoia Lopez joined one of ETA's most ruthless commando cells, which operated from Madrid.

For the previous two years she had taken part in fund-raising exercises – bank robberies, attacks on bars and restaurants – obliging many Basques to pay what ETA likes to call 'revolutionary taxes'. Soon after moving to Madrid, Lopez began to acquire the reputation which would be embellished over the next decade. It was not that she was the only female ETA activist – women have accounted for up to twenty per cent of the organisation's killers – but rather that she looked very striking and was said to have a highly developed libido. The 'Wanted' posters of her, which were visible in Spain for years, showed a pert mouth, large green eyes and thick, tousled black hair. She was known as *La Muelle* ('The Bedspring') and *La Tigressa*, though her lawyer would say that stories of her sexual appetite were made up by the police 'to discredit her, and titillate themselves'.

Just as the convert to Catholicism may be more ardent in following his new-found faith than those who are born to worship in the Church of Rome, so the immigrant Idoia Lopez became more extreme in prosecuting ETA's cause than most committed Basque nationalists. Her enthusiasm may also have had something to do with the fact that she was the lover of the head of the Madrid cell, Juan Manuel Soares. Over the next five years she was involved in some appalling carnage in the capital, including the murder of fourteen members of the Guardia Civil in two separate car-bomb attacks in 1986. There was also the shooting, at point-blank range, of three soldiers and a rocket attack on the defence ministry. Most of the Madrid cell were caught in 1989; Soares escaped to the Dominican republic, and Lopez was removed from Madrid for indiscipline, which was thought to mean too much drinking and sleeping around. One former neighbour remembered her often dressed in black T-shirt and leopard-skin leggings. *La Tigressa* was transferred to a more peripatetic role, making her deadly attacks wherever the ETA high command ordered.

By now she was well-known to the police, and sometimes had to take refuge in France. Until the late 1980s the French Basque country was a reasonably safe haven for ETA terrorists on the run. France liked to be thought of as the land of asylum for political refugees, in particular for 'freedom fighters' from Franco's Spain. The notion persisted long after Franco, to the signal advantage of ETA. Extradition was virtually impossible, and cross-border police cooperation non-existent. The fact that the objective of ETA's campaign of murder and mayhem was to subvert Spain's fledgling democracy seemed to be of no interest to the French. Even after Felipe Gonzalez's Socialists came to power in 1982, President Mitterrand's policy of apparent willingness to harbour fugitives from Spanish justice remained unchanged. It did not help that Mitterrand and Gonzalez did not get on together – the French president preferred the company of the old communist, Santiago Carrillo.

Given no help from its supposedly friendly neighbour, Spain had to take its own measures to contain terrorism. With or without the sanction of government ministers, an anti-terrorist assassination squad, known as GAL (Anti-terrorist Liberation Group) and drawn mainly from the frustrated Guardia Civil, decided it would track down those ETA refugees in south-western France left alone by the French authorities and dispense summary justice on the spot. After all, it would save a lot of time and trouble, and might teach those Frenchmen something about catching criminals. GAL's methods had some success in the early 1980s – twenty-seven ETA members were killed – but the trouble was that its operations were not carried out with the utmost secrecy. When a senior police officer from Bilbao was found to have been using his Visa card on several occasions in the casinos of San Sebastian and Biarritz, questions began to be asked. When the scandal erupted in the press in 1994-5 and accusations were made that even the prime minister might be implicated, no one seemed prepared to say that GAL had done some useful work which had been made necessary by France's refusal to cooperate. Its undercover activities might have been more acceptable in a democracy that had been longer established.

As it turned out, the enormous embarrassment to the Spanish government, in at least tacitly associating itself with criminal illegality, gave ETA a much-needed boost. ETA has always measured its success by the overreaction of the 'enemy'. Tales of torture and deaths in police custody helped the cause in the late 1970s. In 1995 there were stories of slush funds being paid by the interior ministry to Spanish police officers operating in France; and two bodies of ETA activists who had suffered torture were exhumed from a shallow grave outside Alicante. Continuing revelations from an investigating judge and the newspaper *El Mundo*, both of them opposed to the government, were useful to ETA at a time when its fortunes were at a low ebb.

France's official attitude to fugitive terrorists changed after Jacques Chirac became prime minister and appointed Charles Pasqua as interior minister. Procedures were agreed between the two governments for the handover of ETA suspects detained in France, and the Spanish and French police forces at last began to work together. ETA's active list dropped below one hundred, and in 1989 peace talks were held in Algiers with the Spanish security minister. But they got nowhere.

159

Not long afterwards Idoia Lopez was thought to be on the run in Algeria – there are contacts between ETA and Algerian fundamentalists – but by 1991 she had returned to France, where she was to remain in hiding. The following year a joint French-Spanish operation succeeded in arresting most of the executive committee of ETA in the French Pyrenees; but Lopez once again avoided capture. *La Tigressa* was finally cornered near Marseilles in August 1994 while staying with a French boyfriend. He was released but she was taken to a Paris jail to await lengthy extradition procedures. The charges against her relate to twenty-three terrorist killings, for which she may not be tried in Spain until 1998. Meanwhile she lives more comfortably in a French jail, together with other Basque women prisoners, than she would if she were held in Spain.

Lopez's parents still live in grimy, polluted Renteria with their other daughter, and every few weeks they make the journey, by coach, to Paris to visit the daughter described by the Spanish interior ministry when she was arrested as 'a mythical figure of Basque terrorism'. In prison *La Tigressa* practises yoga and writes poetry; but she has not been tamed. She continues to espouse the cause in the same rigid and largely meaningless terms, and with as much vehemence as ever.

Her arrest coincided almost exactly with the IRA ceasefire and the start of the 'peace process' in Northern Ireland. For the next few months violence subsided and there was some hope that ETA might be persuaded to follow the Irish example. When a Basque member of the principal opposition party (Partido Popular) was assassinated in San Sebastian in January 1995, protests and anti-violence marches were widespread throughout the Basque country and a peace group called Elkarri (Together) was formed from among ETA's previous supporters. However, assassination attempts were to be made in 1995 against both Jose Maria Aznar and the King (the latter frustrated thanks to close cooperation between French and Spanish police forces); and in 1997 the murder of a Basque councillor provoked the largest demonstration against violence ever seen in Spain.

The active strength of ETA was by now probably no more than fifty, concentrated in two commando cells, in Guipuzcoa and Madrid. It was no longer an intellectual movement that turned to violence, but a group of disaffected, and probably unemployed, youths who are brainwashed into believing that their war of independence justifies the murder of entirely innocent, and often Basque, women and children. They are too young to have taken up arms against Franco, which was ETA's original purpose, but they come from towns and/or families where the terrorist mentality is deeply ingrained. Apart from Renteria, the most notorious places are within what is called the Death Triangle of Hernani, Villabona and Placencia (see pages 148–9).

Posters and graffiti which I have seen in Hernani, encouraging homosexuality and drug-taking, suggest that today's ETA killers are a very different lot from those of twenty years ago, who had been known on occasion to show their oddly puritanical disapproval of drug dealers by shooting them. There is a parallel here with Northern Ireland. The old-style IRA leadership in the 1970s was devoutly Catholic, and would bomb the only strip club in Belfast. Masturbation among IRA women prisoners in Armagh jail was prohibited by their commander because it was 'unrepublican'. The newer generation of Provos was more cosmopolitan: they had long hair, they smoked dope and – anathema to the old guard – they used condoms. In a similar way the reactionary, ethnic absolutism of the founders of ETA has been replaced by the goal of a socialist state which would be liberated sexually, if in no other way.

The political arm of ETA, however, has little in common with Sinn Fein. Herri Batasuna is strictly controlled by the ETA hierarchy; it has no political leadership, no Gerry Adams figure who straddles the two. If a Herri Batasuna representative is known to have made overtures to, or even contact with, another political party, he is likely to receive a telephone call from an ETA executive advising him to get out of the organisation while he can. After the killing of a Basque politician in January 1995 a rare public protest was made by a Herri Batasuna spokeswoman. But one may imagine that she was not permitted to speak out of turn again.

Though Herri Batasuna's popularity was declining in the 1990s, it was still able to claim around fifteen per cent support in the Basque parliament, with more than a hundred and fifty thousand votes. They come principally from the families and friends of the five hundred or more ETA prisoners and the same number of fugitives, many of whom are living in Cuba, the Dominican republic and the Cape Verde islands. There are also the former members of ETA and the immigrant families for whom extreme radicalism and an adopted nationalism hold a potent appeal. But Herri Batasuna has less to do with nationalism than with hatred, violence and delinquency.

Many of the older Basque nationalists, who might have been drawn to ETA in its early years, stopped voting for Herri Batasuna when its inflammatory rhetoric had little to do with independence for the Basque country. It was getting support from the kind of people who were attracted only by violence and contemptuous of all political parties. What has made ETA/Herri Batasuna perhaps more danger-ous is its changed role. More than anything, it has become a mafia for killing and extortion, because its supposed objective, independence, is not of any concern today to the vast majority of Basques. In a 1994 opinion poll among Basques which asked them to list their priorities, independence came fifteenth. A higher proportion of voters in Scotland wants independence than in the Basque country.

The fact is that Basques have as much autonomy as they want. They raise and collect their own taxes, run their own schools and have their own television and radio channels. They have their own Basque police force, for all matters except terrorism and customs, and they call their towns by Basque names (Gasteiz for Vitoria, the Basque capital; Donostia for San Sebastian) which are listed first on Spanish maps.

One wonders what more can be conceded by the Spanish govern-ment which would persuade ETA to bring its 'armed struggle' to an end. The situation is a depressing one because the armed struggle seems to be pursued merely for its own sake. There are, however, three possible areas for negotiation: prisoners, the Guardia Civil and Navarre. The release of at least some ETA prisoners would be expected following a ceasefire, but the removal of the Guardia Civil from responsibility for terrorism would probably have to await the 'decommissioning' of ETA's arsenal – when the police force would become redundant. Though seldom popular, the Guardia Civil has not been an intrusive or threatening presence in the Basque country;

unlike the situation for many years in Northern Ireland, no outside police or military force patrols the streets of Bilbao or San Sebastian.

Since the Basque police have already proved effective against ETA terrorists, they could surely gradually take over the Guardia Civil's role. More complex, perhaps, is the question of Navarre, which has to do with atavism and the mythology of Arana. Navarrans have no wish to belong to an autonomous Basque state; but to those members of ETA/Herri Batasuna who are genuinely striving for Basque independence, the unification of the four Basque provinces is equally important.

Here, surely, is scope for some imaginative formula, referring to closer cultural, political, economic, etc., ties between the various Basque provinces forming part of an autonomous region within Europe. One Spanish politician, alluding to the Anglo-Irish agreement on the future of Northern Ireland, told me that he envied our talent for drafting politically sensitive documents. The Spanish, he said, were no good at finding the ambiguous phrase which would satisfy two conflicting sides.

Contacts and negotiations, however, will have to start before ETA lays down its arms – a lesson to be learned from the truce negotiated with the IRA in 1994. The difficulty will be in finding a political leader in Herri Batasuna with the courage and authority to persuade ETA to acknowledge that the war is over. Then the time may come, in the foreseeable future, to sell the idea – as with Gibraltar (see pages 183–4), so with the Basque country – of 'autonomy within Europe'.

TWELVE

Rock Not So Solid

The Spanish love talking. In the early evening, which in summer means around 8 pm , they indulge in that most civilised of pastimes, the *paseo*. They go for a stroll, in the streets of their town or village, with no purpose other than to take the air and pass the time of day with whomever they may meet. Every town has its promenade or main street suitable for pedestrians, and every village its central square, where families, lovers and old men can come together to discuss how the day has gone. Idle chatter (*ocio*) may also take place at any time of day, and often in places – the middle of the street or a supermarket – where inconvenience will be caused to people going about their lawful occasions.

For more serious discussion, ostensibly of an intellectual nature, there is the *tertulia*, a gathering in a bar, more in the manner of the coffee-houses of seventeenth-century London. It will usually result in what would be called, in diplomatic language, a lively exchange of views on almost any subject. Informal debate, often noisy, is part of life in Spain, and alcohol helps to give force to differing opinions. But two topics are rarely discussed: the civil war – among older people bitter memories remain while to the young it is history – and, because it is one matter on which everyone is agreed, Gibraltar.

There is no argument among Spaniards about Gibraltar: it is part of the Iberian peninsula, it rightfully belongs to Spain, its status as a British Crown colony is an indefensible anachronism. No *tertulias* are

wasted in debating the subject because they are convinced that, sooner or later, Britain will have to hand the Rock back to Spain. When a foreigner dares to draw parallels with the enclave of Ceuta, on the other side of the Straits – which is part of mainland Morocco but belongs to Spain – he is told in no uncertain terms that the two situations are quite different, because Ceuta, and the town of Melilla along the coast towards Algeria, are parts of metropolitan Spain. (Ten small islands off the Moroccan coast also belong to Spain and are classified as overseas territories. When, during the 1982 Falklands war, Spain supported Argentina's claim to the Falkland Islands, known to people of Iberian descent as Las Malvinas, someone mischievously asked, in an article in *El Pais*, 'How do you say Malvinas in Moroccan?')

Gibraltar was known to the Greeks and Romans as Calpe which, together with the rock called Abyla on the African coast near Ceuta, formed the Pillars of Hercules. The turbulent military history of Gibraltar began with its capture in AD 711 by Tariq-ibn-Ziyad; the name is a corruption of Jebel (Mount) Tariq. The Rock was retaken by Catholic Spain in 1309, but successfully besieged again by the Moors over the next one hundred and fifty years. Uninterrupted Spanish possession then followed for the next two hundred and fifty years, until Gibraltar was captured by British and Dutch forces in 1704. It has been a Crown colony since the Treaty of Utrecht, 1713, with little attempt by Spain to wrest the Rock forcibly from the British since the famous four-year siege towards the end of the eighteenth century.

In the Treaty of Utrecht King Philip V undertook 'for himself, his heirs and successors, [to] yield to the Crown of Great Britain the full and entire propriety of the town and castle of Gibraltar . . . and he gives up the said propriety to be held and enjoyed absolutely with all manner of right for ever, without any exception or impediment whatsoever'. A pretty clear and unequivocal surrender of territory, one might think, which Spain cannot possibly dispute today. The treaty also provided that 'no leave shall be given under any pretence whatsoever either to Jews or Moors to reside . . . in the said town of Gibraltar'.

But that injunction was not obeyed for long. After the Rock had been taken by the British the Spanish population left, most of them to found the town of San Roque about six miles away. New immigrants to Gibraltar came from Malta, Menorca, Genoa and Morocco. By 1750 nearly one third of the population was Jewish. The long-serving former Chief Minister, Sir Joshua Hassan, was able to cock a double snook at the Treaty of Utrecht, since he was both Jewish and of Moroccan descent. By the nineteenth century much intermarrying with Spaniards had taken place, and today all Gibraltarians speak Spanish (albeit as a second language) and ninety per cent of them are Catholic. In 1993, ostensibly to protect jobs of Gibraltarians, who are also British citizens, the eccentric former Chief Minister, Joe Bossano, imposed restrictions on those British citizens living and working in the colony who are not Gibraltarians.

If this sounds like illegal discrimination, that is almost certainly what it was. Other European Community nationals coming to work in Gibraltar – including those from the old enemy, Spain – were not subject to the same restrictions, for instance on the issuing of work permits and entitlement to family income benefit. The Treaty of Rome 'prohibits discrimination by a member state against its own nationals', but here it was being blatantly practised by Gibraltar against its mother country. It is hard to resist the conclusion that Gibraltarian xenophobia embraces both Spain and Britain.

Much of the problem relates to Gibraltar's status within the European Union. It is part of the EU only as a subsidiary of Britain; it has no seat in the European Parliament and remains outside the Customs Union and exempt from VAT. Britain is responsible for enforcing EU directives affecting Gibraltar, and for its external affairs. Mr Bossano said that Gibraltar should be a separate state of the EU, though not completely independent of Britain. He talked about 'the eradication of colonialism' and 'the sacred right to freedom and self-determination', but as philosophical concepts more than practical goals. Gibraltarianism is widely spoken of, Gibraltar Day is celebrated with red and white Gibraltar flags far outnumbering Union Jacks, and people refer these days to Gibraltar's identity as a nation. This is all very well, but the vast majority of Gibraltarians also wish to retain the link with Britain – and their British citizenship. The reason is simple, and explains why no Chief Minister, will ever call for Gibraltar's independence. The Treaty of Utrecht provides that if Britain should relinquish sovereignty over the Rock, it shall pass to Spain. When a referendum was held among Gibraltarians in 1967, on a ninety-six per cent turnout forty-four voted for association with

Spain and 12,138 for continuing the existing link with Britain. That was two years before Franco closed the frontier – which was to stay shut for the next sixteen years. A similar referendum held today would not produce a very different result.

I have interviewed Mr Bossano twice, the first time in 1980 when he was leader of the Gibraltar Socialist Labour party and branch officer of the Transport and General Workers' Union. It was shortly after the British and Spanish governments had issued one of those joint statements which have the advantage of being capable of different interpretation by both sides. The communiqué, signed in Lisbon while Gibraltar's frontier with Spain was still closed, did not mention sovereignty by name, but made it clear that Britain would continue to 'honour the freely and democratically expressed wishes of the people of Gibraltar'. It also spoke of 'future cooperation on the basis of reciprocity and full equality of rights'.

If that meant freedom for Spaniards to come and work on the Rock, Mr Bossano was having none of it. 'We shall continue to exercise very tight control over the number of Spaniards we allow to work here,' he said. 'And they will be required to join the TGWU. Never in my lifetime will we accept the presence of Spanish unions here.' My principal memory of that interview was being kept waiting in an outer office of Gibraltar's Transport House which I was obliged to share with a Dobermann pinscher. The previous month the printing staff of the *Gibraltar Chronicle* had stopped work one afternoon and refused to resume until they had spoken to Mr Bossano. It emerged later that the action was taken in order to remonstrate with the TGWU branch officer for having failed to keep three appointments with the editor. (He only missed one appointment with me.)

At our second interview, in 1994, Joe Bossano was sitting at the head of a table when I was ushered in, with a recording machine on one side of him and a copy of an article I had written six months earlier in the *Sunday Telegraph* on the other. His opening remarks were not welcoming, though I had scarcely expected that they would be. 'You've been Gibraltar-bashing; don't you think I should bash you?' Risking the wrath of the notoriously truculent leader of Britain's only Mediterranean colony, I replied that I had only been bashing

Bossano, not Gibraltar. He managed a smile.

It is hard indeed to acquit Mr Bossano of blame for Gibraltar's recent economic plight. Following his election as Chief Minister in 1988, he initiated a huge development project in the docks by reclaiming land from the sea. In a series of joint ventures, many of them with Danish money, apartment and office blocks, and a building components factory, were constructed. The factory was soon abandoned, the Hyatt group pulled out of a hotel and business complex, and in 1995 no more than ten per cent of the development was occupied. One of the few signs of life, when I last went there, was the Duck and Firkin pub. Property prices in Spain were more than fifty per cent lower, while tourism in Gibraltar declined in the early 1990s: the occupancy rate for the Rock's thirteen hundred hotel beds was less than thirty per cent in 1993. Gibraltar failed to develop as an offshore finance centre to the extent that had been anticipated – in part because of a dispute with the British government over the appointment of a Financial Services Commissioner – and business closures increased at a disconcerting rate. Gibraltarians took the opportunity not only to buy property in Spain but also to cross the frontier to do their supermarket shopping more cheaply in La Linea.

Mr Bossano would say that Gibraltar's problems were caused by the withdrawal of the Ministry of Defence following the closure of the naval dockyards and the consequent loss of jobs and support to the economy. He blamed the British government for failing to protect the economic stability of Gibraltar, for which, he said, it is ultimately responsible. But there was plenty for which Mr Bossano himself was responsible. He refused to implement a 1987 agreement between Britain and Spain for joint use of the airport, which remained open only to a couple of British airlines running services between England, Gibraltar and Morocco. Negotiations for an air service between Gibraltar and Portugal did not make much progress. During his second term – Mr Bossano was returned in elections in 1992 with seventy-three per cent of the vote – the Socialist Chief Minister became something of a Thatcherite, privatising water, the telephone and the companies registry. He also became less answerable to Parliament, which met only about twice a year.

Meanwhile, to shore up government revenues and to compensate for income lost through unemployment, Gibraltar indulged in smuggling. In the early 1990s the government was receiving more than £10 million a year in duty on imported cigarettes, ninety per cent of which were exported illegally to Spain. The smugglers were known as the Winston Boys (after the brand of cigarette most commonly sold to Spain) and their 70 mph rigid inflatable boats (RIBs) with Zodiac engines were well known to everyone in Gibraltar. To a lesser extent, they were also said to be used for drug-running between Morocco and Spain. The government seemed reluctant to do anything to curb this illegal trade, not least, it was rumoured, because there were ministers who had shares in some of the boats and their proceeds.

Spain responded by making life tiresome at the border crossing for those going into or out of Gibraltar. The long delays brought about by Spanish officials, for no justifiable reason, were especially frustrating for those people living in Spain and commuting daily to work on the Rock. At the same time Spain complained to the British Foreign Office, not only about the smuggling but about allegations of money laundering by companies registered in Gibraltar. This was thought by some to be a bit rich – financial malpractice is, after all, not unknown among Spanish ministers and public officials and far more drugs are imported from Morocco through Ceuta than via Gibraltar – but it gave the Foreign Office the excuse to bash Mr Bossano.

Here one could sympathise with Gibraltar's then Chief Minister. He denied being anti-British, but he could hardly be blamed for being anti-Foreign Office – which would be much relieved to be rid of the Gibraltar problem, even if it meant handing the Rock back to Spain. Of course, the Foreign Office insists that Britain remains committed to the 1969 constitution and that no deal will be made behind Gibraltar's back. But Mr Bossano could be forgiven for having his doubts. 'I see it as a sort of parental relationship,' he told me. 'The UK should be fighting my corner, not screwing me to protect itself in Brussels.'

In 1995, however, the British government did 'screw' Mr Bossano into acting against the smugglers and agreeing to implement EU directives, some of which related to financial regulation and which Britain was responsible for enforcing. When Gibraltar police impounded about sixty RIBs, the tobacco smugglers reacted by staging a riot in protest at this unwarranted restriction on their livelihood. Thinking they were, in effect, beyond the law, they set fire to a police car and broke a police officer's leg. Anarchy threatened, but a few days later eight thousand non-smugglers came out on to Main Street in support of the police. It was the largest demonstration in Gibraltar that anyone could remember. The importing of RIBs was banned, though no one was under any illusion that the tobacco run would come to an end. There was no shortage of speedboats left in the harbour.*

One night I went to dinner at a fish restaurant just outside La Linea, on the coast road. We took a table in the window, hoping to see a bit of action. This was one of the tobacco beaches, and a drop was expected. No excitements had occurred, however, by the time we left the restaurant, so I had to rely on the account of one of my companions who had witnessed a drop the previous week. The Guardia Civil would have only a few moments to make an arrest or intercept the contraband, from the time it was dumped ashore until it was rushed across the road and into the tenement buildings behind the restaurant. Once there, it could be safely hidden in flats which the authorities usually treated as 'no-go' areas. The crime rate in La Linea, due mainly to drugs and unemployment, is one of the highest in Spain. In the Plaza del Pintor Cruz Herrera, where on a Saturday night the microskirts worn by the young *guapas* seemed to have risen to disturbing new heights, the blare of an English pop song came from one of the bars: 'Running around my brain, I've got cocaine . . . ' On the way back to the frontier, I was accosted by two ageing prostitutes.

On the Rock, the Gibraltarians take a puritan satisfaction in being free of such vices. It may be one of the most famous ports in the Mediterranean, but Gibraltar fails to provide sailors with one of the staple pleasures of a run ashore – sex for sale. I was in Gibraltar in February 1994, when the aircraft carrier *Ark Royal* called in for two days, on her way to the Adriatic to be ready for the possibility of air

* Since the election of Peter Caruana as Chief Minister in 1996, Gibraltar has gone some way towards shedding its reputation as a centre for drugs smuggling and money laundering.

171

strikes against the Bosnian Serbs. At morning service on Sunday in the King's Chapel, adjoining the sixteenth-century convent which serves as the Governor's residence, *Ark Royal's* chaplain spoke in his sermon of the delights of a run ashore at Gibraltar, quoting from Ecclesiastes ix: 7 – 'Go thy way, eat thy bread with joy and drink thy wine with a merry heart.'

I had seen hordes of sailors the night before, eating very little except for packets of crisps but drinking large quantities of English beer, which in Gibraltar pubs is served much too cold. They seemed merry enough, on one of their last nights ashore for several months, but something was missing. One would not have expected Ecclesiastes to mention it, but sailors the world over, when they are in port, are accustomed to expect a little female company – a few moments with a prostitute in a dark alley or an upstairs room, or at least the sight of a bit of bare flesh in some back-street bar. In Gibraltar, however, our boys had to do without it.

They walked the length of Main Street, down the narrow lanes off Irish Town, along Line Wall Road overlooking the dockyard, but to no avail. There were countless pubs – the Clipper, Three Owls, Angry Friar, Horseshoe – but not a loose woman in sight. Nor is there a live show, a striptease club or even an 'adult' magazine to be found. In this last Mediterranean outpost of the British Empire, a run ashore is not all it should be.

The man apparently responsible for depriving the Royal Navy of a little much-needed relaxation before the rigours of a spell of duty on the high seas was the Roman Catholic Bishop of Gibraltar. A few years back, he learnt that *Playboy* magazine had published photographs of a Miss Gibraltar without her clothes on and he decided to act – operating an informal censorship of all clubs and permitting *Playboy* and similar publications to be sold only at the airport.

Some Gibraltar residents talked nostalgically of the days of the Trocadero and the 21 Club, where young ladies were available, also of Uncle Tom's Cabin, part of which used to be run as a gentleman's club and brothel. Gib Liz was well-known for years to visitors and residents, but she had long since retired. The irony was that, while this aspect of Gibraltarian life had been closed down at the behest of a

Catholic bishop, a mile away across the border in Catholic Spain the crew of *Ark Royal*, had they had the time and thought to bring their passports, could have enjoyed all manner of sexual services. Apart from the brothels of La Linea, the English-language edition of *Sur* regularly carries at least a column of classified advertisements for 'Adult Relaxation', including temptations such as 'Transvestites, well hung, big breasts. Novelties. Hygiene Control'.

Perhaps the sailors did not know what they were missing. When one beer-filled Scottish rating, who had been wolf-whistling a Moroccan woman in a djellaba, asked me, 'Where the fuck do you have to go to get a fuck round here?' I thought it kinder not to mention the exotic but inaccessible attractions that lay just across the border. I asked him instead what he thought about the prospect of hostilities in the Adriatic. With what at the time seemed to be a witty, if unintended, evocation of George V's words on his deathbed, he answered, 'Bugger Bosnia' and disappeared down Ragged Staff Road towards the enfolding embrace of *Ark Royal*.

Two centuries ago naval officers and seamen in Gibraltar were quite likely to die, if not in battle, of Malignant Fever, as recorded on many headstones in the Trafalgar Cemetery. A tablet in the King's Chapel commemorates a junior officer who in 1804 died of 'a fatal pestilential disorder'. Life was chancier then, but at least there was female company to be had on the Rock. For our young sailors from *Ark Royal*, spending two nights ashore before going possibly to war, the only pleasure to be had was from a can of cold Worthington or a pint of draught lager.

Gibraltar may have reason to boast about its sexual cleanliness but not, from the evidence of my last two visits, about the state of its streets. True, there was a strike of refuse workers on one occasion – bags of rubbish rotting in the streets at 90°F – but Gibraltar does appear to have a more general problem with litter, and with derelict cars. However, it is not as bad as it was in the last century. In his *Handbook for Travellers in Spain*, Richard Ford warned of an unidentified plague which struck the Rock about once every twelve years and was called 'Gibraltar Fever': 'It is nurtured in Hebrew dirt, fed by want of circulation of air and offensive sewers at low tide. It is called into fatal activity by some autumnal atmospherical activity.' It was almost certainly a form of yellow fever carried by mosquitoes.

This may have been the fatal pestilential disorder which caused the death of the officer commemorated in the King's Chapel, or the Malignant Fever inscribed in the Trafalgar Cemetery. This is one of the most charming, as well as historically important, places in Gibraltar. The graves of those British ensigns and lieutenants who died after the great battle are now partly grown over with peculiarly English flowers – pelargoniums, nasturtiums and irises. In the King's Chapel (the forces' church) the font is made of grey marble from the *sierra* behind Malaga; Mass is celebrated here every Saturday evening, beneath a large stained glass window depicting a former head of the Church of England, King George VI. The Anglican cathedral down the road has Moorish windows.

Oddities in Gibraltar are not hard to find. One day I saw some Russian sailors drinking pints of Bass outside the Angry Friar. They were watching bemused as a group of Moroccans arrived in Convent Place, outside the Chief Minister's office, to begin their daily demonstration. 'In some countries there are racist people. In Gibraltar it is the Government' read one placard, and another, 'Gibraltar Government worst in Europe'. Moroccans are very much at the bottom of the heap: they receive no benefits, and if they lose their jobs are unlikely to be re-employed.

The most distinguished of all Gibraltarians, a Jew of Moroccan descent, was employed as Chief Minister for the best part of forty years. The career of Sir Joshua Abraham Hassan, CBE, MVO, QC, JP is not without its curiosities. He was educated at the Christian Brothers College in Gibraltar, but did not change his religion. He did, however, change the law so that he could divorce his Spanish wife and marry a Moroccan. Catholic Gibraltar allowed divorce only on grounds of adultery; Sir Joshua, wishing to divorce his wife for cruelty and desertion, introduced a Bill in the Legislative Council in 1969 to allow him, and only him, to end his marriage in this way. The Council , and then the British Foreign Secretary, duly gave their approval. When I first met Sir Joshua, he invited me to his chambers. Most remarkably, he practised as a lawyer in the morning and ran the government in the afternoon. 'We have a code of conduct to cover that,' he told me reassuringly. 'And anyway, government should not be full-time.' He was still in practice as a lawyer at the age of eighty, having enriched himself, it was said, largely through setting up and administering tax-haven companies in Gibraltar for a number of shady clients, and was still in practice as a lawyer until shortly before he died, aged 81, in 1997.

When Sir Joshua walked up Main Street he was greeted, often with affection, as the distinguished elderly figure which he unquestionably was. Every Saturday morning he would spend a couple of hours at Sir Winston's Tavern, where people knew they could have a word with him, perhaps to seek assurance about Gibraltar's future. When I called to see him one day, he was sitting beneath a picture of Churchill, which carried the inscription: 'Let Us Go Forward Together'.

Togetherness for Gibraltarians means standing united in their resistance to Spain, though there is not much evidence of going forward. Most Gibraltarians acknowledge that because of their origins – whether Genoese, Maltese, Spanish or Moroccan – they are essentially Mediterranean, a hybrid product of different cultures. 'But I think in an Anglo-Saxon way,' Mr Bossano, educated at Birmingham and London universities, once told me. 'The UK is less of a foreign country to me than Spain, whose culture I don't understand.'

It is hard to believe this of some Gibraltarians, particularly those with Spanish names, who may have relations living in Spain. There are many notable examples: the secretary-general of Gibraltar's Olympic committee in 1992, Nigel Pardo, shares his surname with the palace in Madrid where Franco had his residence; and the president of the Gibraltar Teachers' Association in 1995, Stephen Linares, shares his with a town in Andalusia where the bullfighter Manolete was killed. The vast majority of Gibraltarians also speak Spanish and are Catholic. But, whether with justification or not, they feel insecure and fear being taken over by Spain; they would rather entrust their security and their future to Britain. No doubt many feel reassured to recall Lord Palmerston bringing out the gunboats on behalf of the Portuguese Jewish merchant Don Pacifico. As a Gibraltar-born British subject, he was entitled, in the words of Queen Victoria's foreign secretary, to 'feel confident that the watchful eye and the strong arm of England will protect him against injustice and wrong'. Perhaps it is still comforting to feel that strong arm – of the policemen dressed as British bobbies? – though one wonders where the injustice and wrong are going to come from. After all, Spain is a rather more civilised country these days; but it sometimes seems as if the Gibraltarians don't want to know. Undoubtedly they retain a siege mentality, long after the reopening of the frontier in 1985. It was those sixteen years of isolation that enormously strengthened the Gibraltarians' sense of identity.

There is very little official contact between Gibraltar and Spain. Mr Bossano told me he kept in touch with the mayors of La Linea and Algeciras, but he admitted to having been only once to mainland Spain in the previous six months (to San Roque) and once to Ceuta. (Mr Caruana crosses the border more often, to visit relatives in Sotogrande and play golf.) Relations were much more cordial in the last century. Even when Britain and Spain were at war, wrote an officer stationed on the Rock, it was 'a common thing, after an attack by the Spaniards on British vessels entering or leaving Gibraltar, for the opposing officers to meet at dinner at the table of either the British or Spanish general'.

Not long after Trafalgar, the birthday of King George III was celebrated with fireworks in Tarifa and Ceuta, and Ferdinand VII's birthday was marked by a royal salute on the Rock, with the Spanish ensign flying above Signal House. Good relations between Gibraltar and Spain used to be particularly in evidence during royal visits. When Queen Adelaide, widow of William IV, spent a few days at Gibraltar in 1838, she rode out to the Spanish cork woods accompanied by an escort of Spanish lancers provided by the Governor of Algeciras. King George V and Queen Mary, calling at Gibraltar in 1912 on their way back from the Delhi Durbar, received King Alfonso XIII's eldest son, who sailed across the bay from Algeciras.

Nothing like this can happen nowadays. If the Queen decided to visit her colony it would cause an international incident. She may meet her third cousin, King Juan Carlos, in London or Madrid, but a meeting on the Rock of Gibraltar would be out of the question. When the Prince and Princess of Wales took the unusually insensitive decision to begin their honeymoon from Gibraltar, on the royal yacht *Britannia*, King Juan Carlos had no alternative but to decline his invitation to the wedding.

Foxhunting provided the best example of Anglo-Spanish cooperation in Gibraltar. For one hundred and twenty-five years a pack of hounds, kennelled on the Rock, would hunt the fox – and sometimes deer and wild boar – over Andalusian country extending from San Roque and Los Barrios north to Castellar. Known as the Calpe Hunt, it became 'Royal' in 1906 when the Kings of England and Spain became its joint patrons. Alfonso XIII remained as patron until hunting came to an end in 1939, though for the last eight years he was in exile.

The Reverend Mark Mackereth, chaplain to the Governor of Gibraltar (then Prince Edward, Duke of Kent) is credited with having founded the hunt in 1813. At first hunting took place on the Upper Rock, where plenty of foxes were to be found; but the pack, of English foxhounds which had arrived by way of Cadiz, was soon hunting the cork woods and olive groves across the border. After the part just played by Britain in expelling the hated French invader from the peninsula, the Spanish were more than happy to let the officers of the Gibraltar garrison indulge their curious passion over the open countryside behind La Linea.

The Calpe was essentially a British hunt, depending always for its survival on maintaining friendly relations with local Spanish landowners and farmers. In his invaluable history of the hunt, *Hounds are Home*, Gordon Fergusson appends a map of the hunting country in which features are identified, mostly with English names – Mansels Thicket, Railway Covert, Herringbone Crags, The Briars, Magazine Hill. Meets were often at the Duke of Kent's Farm (which he had bought for his French mistress); hunting reports could just as well describe a day in Leicestershire, but for the occasional inclusion of a Spanish name on the map which, untranslated, sounds oddly out of place.

Ran from near Woodcock Covert in blinding rain in five-and-half-mile ring via Fern Valley, Little White House, Bailey's Bank and Pinar de Bigotas along the Miraflores track to Pablo's Gorse.

177

The Pablo was Pablo Geronimo Larios who, more than anyone, was responsible for keeping hunting going on Spanish soil. There were several British connections: daughters of the family had married English and Irish officers, the young Pablo had been partly educated in England in the 1880s, and he had hunted in Yorkshire and the Cotswolds. Most significantly, the Larios family owned huge estates along the south coast: it was said that you could ride from Los Barrios to Marbella without leaving Larios land. It was obvious that the Calpe needed to keep on good terms with the Larios family; not only were they easily the largest landowners of the country hunted, but the hunt also depended on one or other Larios to sort out difficulties with local farmers.

There were five brothers, all keen sportsmen, and Pablo had ridden with the Calpe since he was eleven years old. He had been first whipper-in for eight seasons when in 1891 the mastership became vacant. The tradition was that the Master should be a British officer; however, with the active support of the Governor, Pablo Larios was elected. His term was originally restricted to two years – showing some reluctance on the part of the hunt committee to let a Spaniard take over for too long? – but he was to remain in the job, with a short break, until he died in 1938.

In 1903 Pablo Larios built himself a house at Guadacorte, some six miles from Gibraltar between the Guadarranque and Palmones rivers, which looks from one side as if it should be in Scotland, and on the other like an Edwardian retirement home outside Bournemouth. (It was subsequently sold to the Marquess of Bute.) Three years later Larios approached the palace in Madrid, and the hunt committee wrote to Edward VII, to petition both kings to become joint patrons of the hunt. 'The immense importance of such an institution to Your Majesty's subjects who are quartered in or are inhabitants of this Fortress cannot be overrated,' the committee enthused. Their majesties were both pleased to accord their patronage, the hunt became known as the Royal Calpe Hunt and the crowns of England and Spain were added to the hunt buttons. There was great rejoicing when, in the same year, King Alfonso married Princess Ena, a granddaughter of Queen Victoria.

The halcyon days of the Royal Calpe, and by extension of the relationship between Spain and Gibraltar, lasted for the next quarter of a century. New points of reference appeared on the hunting map – each king had a gorse covert named after him – and a photograph of a meet in 1907 shows a mounted field of more than sixty. Hunting did not have to stop for the First World War – Spain was not involved – but the Calpe was proud to record three VCs awarded to its members. When hunt steeplechases were held on the Larios estate, special excursions were offered to Gibraltar residents, by steamer to Algeciras, then on to Guadacorte by train.

Problems began after King Alfonso abdicated and Spain was proclaimed a republic. Hunting was stopped; 'a prudent decision', Gordon Fergusson comments in *Hounds are Home*, 'as within a few weeks the Communist mob vent its destructive fury on the churches of Algeciras, Los Barrios and La Linea'. Hunting was soon resumed, but it was a poor season: poachers were roaming the countryside and the foxes were driven to the hills. Care had to be exercised, especially as no one associated with the Royal Calpe Hunt was likely to be mistaken for a left-wing republican. A daughter of Pablo and Pepita Larios would shortly marry Miguel Primo de Rivera, son of the dictator general of the 1920s and brother of José Antonio, the founder of the Falangist party.

While Spain was lurching from one government to another and towards the nightmare of civil war, the Calpe was having its own not so minor struggle, between the ageing Master, Pablo Larios (now the Marques de Marzales) and the Governor, General Sir Alexander ('Lord God') Godley. Godley, who was not noted for his tact, thought and said it was high time that a young British officer took over from Larios; he was too old and the sport in recent seasons had been disappointing. The hunt 'was in danger of becoming altogether too Spanish, and too civilian an affair'. Larios resigned, a new Master was appointed for the 1932–3 season and the hunt found itself warned off much of its hunting country. When Godley retired in 1933, King George V, as patron, made it clear that he was not impressed by the general's handling of this sorry affair.

Indeed the king threatened to withdraw his patronage unless the new Governor, General Sir Charles Harington, made it up with Larios – which, after some prevarication, he did. The feud was settled by the appointment of Lady Harington and Pablo Larios, Marques de Marzales, as joint masters. They were to share the mastership for the next four years, until Larios's death, but by then the Calpe's days were nearly over.

It was surprising enough that hunting continued at all during the civil war. It did come to a halt for most of the 1936–7 season, but General Harington remained sanguine for the future. 'Everything at the moment looks as if the Whites will get the upper hand in this unfortunate civil war. If they do, things in this neighbourhood will settle down quietly . . . ' Permission was given by the military commandant in Algeciras for the hounds to be exercised in Spain, but the only fox killed during the season was an unfortunate animal that was caught in a trap on the Rock and then thrown to the hounds. It was not in the best traditions of foxhunting; but there was a civil war on, and sporting standards momentarily slipped.

There was no doubt where the sympathies of the hunt lay in this war – though some were upset to hear the nationalist execution squads at night on the Campamento polo ground, where they tied their victims to posts in the pony lines. But things soon quietened down, and by the start of the next season the Governor decided to seek permission from Franco, which he was delighted to grant, to resume hunting two days a week. They were to keep away from the 'war zone', where Red brigands were still at large, but this was poor hunting country, so nobody minded. A Labour MP raised the matter of contacts with Franco in the House of Commons, but was told by the Foreign Secretary, Anthony Eden, that the Royal Calpe Hunt's arrangements with the insurgent nationalists were 'a purely local affair'. It was good to be hunting again, but from more than forty days during the 1937–8 season, only one fox was killed. Old Pablo Larios was not able to continue hunting after February, and he died in April, just before the end of the season.

The war continued to impinge on the Calpe's activities in small ways. Anti-communist feelings, still running high following the capture of most of Andalusia by the nationalists, occasionally fastened on those members of the hunt whose red coats were thought by some locals to denote their political allegiance. When a man once shouted abuse at the 'Red' hunt servants hacking past his cottage, Lady Harington, whose ignorance of the Spanish language was notorious, was said to have thanked him for giving the hunt such a rousing welcome back after its enforced absence due to the war. A painting by Gerald Hare at this time shows the hunt about to cross the Los Barrios-Jerez road, with the nationalist slogan, '*Arriba España!*' painted white on the tarmac. The same words were scratched on the back of a hunt trailer at the end of one January day in 1939 to mark the fall of Barcelona. Any lingering doubts about which side the Calpe 'Reds' were on would have been dispelled when they joined in a celebration with Spanish soldiers.

It was all very well for the hunt to back the winning side while it was still fighting to win, but once Franco had achieved victory over the communist-backed Republic, his decided leanings towards Hitler and the imminence of world war made the continuation of the Royal Calpe Hunt on Spanish soil politically unacceptable. The new Governor of Gibraltar, General Sir Edmund Ironside, who by 1939 had become the Calpe's joint master with Larios's son Pepito (a pilot with the nationalist airforce, he married the Duchess of Lerma), once commented: 'I sometimes wonder what would happen if war broke out on a hunting day. I hope to God it never does, for the Rock could be taken in a matter of minutes.' But there would be no more hunting days after April 1939. Gibraltar was not invaded, but plans to take the Rock were prepared in detail by Hitler, with Franco's cooperation. Once hunting had been finally brought to an end, the twenty-four couple of hounds had to be put down. By the time the kennel huntsman on the Rock, José Pecino, went to join his family in Spain in 1942, after forty-two years' employment with the hunt, nine hounds still remained. One bitch, Vixen, was spared and allowed to die of old age.

An article in *The Times* in 1930, on taking the hounds with Pecino across the frontier for a morning's exercise, gives the flavour of hunting life as it used to be. From the North Front kennels, with the sun just touching the Spanish hills, they made their way towards the border which was in chilly shadow. 'The policeman stopped the ingoing stream of gharries and black-shawled women, the sentry saluted and hounds pattered on to the neutral ground. The ponies capered across the sand. Behind them the Rock towered rosily against the morning. As they cantered along the beach children scattered from their hoofs like coveys of partridges . . . The Spanish sentry, bristling with weapons, grinned at them as they clattered over the cobbles into La Linea.'

One or two hounds darted into a doorway, another chased an old woman with a basket. On the edge of town 'they passed fields where slow oxen drew ploughs that the Moors might have left behind . . . A horseman drew up to let them pass . . . The sun rose into the blue air that was not bluer than the distant cork woods, as they halted at the inn to drink a glass of coffee. The lieutenant turned his pony.

' "Pecino, next Tuesday meet at Second Venta," he said, gazing into his henchman's face like a mesmerist. "Therefore we leave kennel at ten horos and a half, eh?"

' "Si, si señor. Second Venta very goo', plenty foc." '

There have been times when, thinking about the Gibraltar problem, I have wistfully imagined that the best first step towards a resolution would be to revive the Royal Calpe Hunt, again under the joint patronage of the monarchs of England and Spain. But I fear it wouldn't work: the British officers are not there any more, the sport would appeal to very few Gibraltarians, and it would hardly be practical nowadays, to say the least, to keep the hounds kennelled on the Rock. A small hunt called the Guadiaro was established in 1978 in the Andalusian hills behind Sotogrande, for British expatriate and Spanish residents; but the link with Gibraltar has gone for ever.

What, then, can one say of Gibraltar's future? At the Gibraltar Day celebrations in 1993, Joe Bossano appeared to align himself with a faction demanding independence for Catalonia. A Catalan guest speaker referred to Gibraltar as having, like Catalonia, a 'national identity as a nation'. The wily old president of the regional government of Catalonia, Jordi Pujol, may not have gone so far as to call for complete independence, but he has spoken of Catalonia as 'a nation in Spain and Europe', and has called for a greater devolution of powers than was granted by the autonomy statute of 1980. The Chief Minister would not claim outright independence for Gibraltar, but as much independence as possible to run its own affairs and play a more direct role in Europe – for instance by being represented in European elections. Is it not possible also to envisage Gibraltar as 'a nation in Europe', while under the aegis of both Britain and Spain?

The Foreign Office has acknowledged that joint sovereignty is on the agenda as a way of resolving Gibraltar's future status – this would at least stop Spain continuing, almost as a matter of course, to obstruct Gibraltar in Brussels. The more acceptable solution may be to follow the example of Andorra, giving Gibraltar virtual independence, and membership of the United Nations, subject to a joint role for Britain and Spain as 'co-principals'.

Mr Bossano used to argue for the integration of Gibraltar with Britain, but even he came to accept that this would provoke Spain unduly and possibly beyond all hope of ever resolving the Gibraltar problem. It has to be remembered, after all, that for Spain Gibraltar is *the* foreign affair. What many Gibraltarians object to strongly is being classified as a dependent territory. Understandably enough, they want to retain a link with Britain but without the colonial connection – which has been steadily weakened by the decline of the British military presence on the Rock and the withdrawal of Ministry of Defence personnel. The larger the proportion of heterogeneous Gibraltarians, the easier it should be, in many respects, to reach an accommodation with Spain.

For if Spain can accept the autonomy of its regions within Spain, it is surely not inconceivable that it could come to accept the autonomy of Gibraltar within Europe and under the carefully negotiated joint authority – a more acceptable word to Gibraltarians than sovereignty – of Britain and Spain. As with most negotiations, it is a question of what can be achieved with the minimum loss of face by, in this case, all three parties. Now that so many Spanish banks and commercial companies are contributing to Gibraltar's economy, it can only be a matter of time before political relations follow. If the Basques can retain their language and culture and are allowed a substantial degree of self-government, what do the Gibraltarians have to fear?

Some such autonomy status will surely be the outcome for what I once called, perhaps a little unfairly, 'that embarrassing wart on the bottom of the Iberian peninsula'; the only question is when. In 1997, for the first time, a Governor, Sir Richard Luce, was appointed who was a politician rather than a retired senior British officer. Perhaps that may have been the first step towards the lowering of the Union Jack on the roof of the sixteenth-century convent which is his residence – and its replacement by the white and red-striped flag of Gibraltar, with its red castle and key hanging from the gateway.

THIRTEEN

Back to the Hills

Above the south-east coast, in the province of Almeria, stands the Moorish hill village of Mojacar. From below it has an undeniably Arab aspect – its white buildings squat, flat-roofed and seemingly on top of one another – and in its narrow streets women veiled their faces little more than thirty years ago. In the Sixties many of the local residents left – over much of Spain it was a time of migration away from rural districts – to be replaced by artists and, later, incoming *ingleses* of a certain age. Mojacar's Moorish past survives in its architecture and in the couscous on the menu at El Moresco; while Mohacker's uncompromisingly British present thrives at El Antler, the sign of the stag, where Stuart and Sharon welcome their customers every evening from seven o'clock.

Covering the walls are framed posters and advertisements: one for a chemist's in Cheltenham, another for North Sea Heavy Dark Old Rum, from John E. McPherson of Leith. There are old locks and taps, a brass gong, a Watneys plaque, and pictures of deer. Sharon was talking about poor old Lofty's diabetes; she had been to see him along the coast in Nerja. I asked for a glass of sherry, but they only had the sweet. When Doris came in with a white poodle on a lead, the conversation turned to the line dancing classes at Kuki's pub on the beach. A card on the wall announced the month's programme for the Almeria Lawn Bowling Club, with a special mention for the inaugural British Legion event. In Stuart and Sharon's restaurant

185

next to the bar, an elderly couple were finishing their evening meal at 8.30, at least an hour before any Spaniard would think of starting dinner. Shaking my head in amused disbelief, I walked along the cobbled street, overhung with dark balconies, to the church of Santa Maria, where two people called Gershwin were giving a concert of *musica sacra*.

Next morning I walked down the hill to the marbled Arab courtyard and fountain where local women still bring their washing. One old lady hitched up her skirt, removed her stockings, put on a waterproof apron and stood in water up to her knees, rubbing the clothes on a stone slab in front of her. Above her head a large plaque records that here, in 1488, the last Moorish mayor of Mojacar, Alavez, met the envoy of Ferdinand and Isabella, Garcilaso. The inscription records the words of Alavez – that he had never taken up arms against the Christians, that he would declare his loyalty to the Catholic monarchs, and that in return he expected to be left in peace. But if it came to a fight, 'rather than surrender like a coward I will know how to die like a Spaniard. May Allah protect you!' Garcilaso replied with offers of friendship: 'we accede to your demand having heard your noble reasoning . . . May God save you and all your people!' As far as we know, Alavez was left unharmed.

At the bottom of the hill, along the coast road, unreality intruded again. Snoopy's British Bar & Diner was offering a Sunday lunch of roast pork, roast potatoes, stuffing and apple sauce, while next door Dave and Sheila at Los Amigos advertised Tetley Bitter and the lottery numbers. It was time to head far inland.

I hurried past the 'Spaghetti Western' film sets of Fort Bravo and Yucca City, set in desert landscape near Tabernas (and now marked on maps as Mini Hollywood). Into the sierras and beyond Baza, great red sandstone crags stood above the reservoir of Negratin; deep canyons fell away below the dam. After Pozo Alcon the scenery becomes even wilder and more dramatic, as the narrow road climbs steeply to where only yellow broom grows out of the rock-face and the Devon-red soil of the desolate hillside. Near the top of the pass the road twists through pine forests to the tiny village of Tiscar, where a sanctuary sits almost impossibly high up on the pinnacle of a crag. A few miles to the north, over a couple of 6,000-foot peaks, a spring issues forth from a jumble of rocks to become what the Moors called the Great River of Spain.

The River Guadalquivir is in fact the shortest, at 360 miles, of the Big Five (Ebro, Tagus, Douro and Guadiana are the others). But it is more Spanish than the Tagus, Douro and Guadiana, which also flow through Portugal, and it has two great, originally Roman, cities, Sevilla and Cordoba, along its banks (the Ebro has only Saragossa). The Guadalquivir was navigable to ships as far as Cordoba when that city was the Moorish capital of Spain, and during the time of the New World conquests it was used by the treasure ships returning across the Atlantic Ocean to Seville. *Nacimiento*, or birthplace, is the word for the source of a river; where the Guadalquivir is born, I thought, is surely the womb, if not the heart, of Spain.

To get there I knew I would have to walk the last few kilometres; the road ends at the Puente de las Herrerias, a fifteenth-century bridge supposedly built for Queen Isabella to cross the infant river with her forces marching south to Granada. Having spent the night outside Cazorla, I woke to a morning of low cloud, heavy rain and wind. It was, as the manager of the hotel informed me, a *tormenta*. The road continued uphill and visibility deteriorated to a few yards as the swirling cloud seemed almost to envelop the car. An old man with an umbrella appeared out of the gloom. I had read somewhere that this sierra was very popular for thrush shooting, but no birds were flying or calling today. The birthplace of the Guadalquivir was somewhere ahead, but water was everywhere around, pouring down the hillsides and across the road. Fallen boulders and pine tree branches were also making progress hazardous; it was becoming clear − if nothing else around me was − that this journey of discovery would have to be postponed. Later that day, down in the valley, I crossed the brown, swollen and fast-running river. Heavy with rain, branches of the poplars along its banks were bent low over the water.

The landscape was covered, as I could see when the clouds lifted, by olive trees, serried ranks of them undulating in endless lines all over the hillsides. Were the armies of the Moors and Christians so orderly, I wondered, as they faced one another before the Battle of Las Navas

187

de Tolosa in 1212? After Alfonso VIII's famous victory – the site is a few miles north of Linares – the Arabs were soon driven out of the cities of Jaen and Ubeda. The Moorish legacy here was not considered so sacrosanct; little is left today apart from an occasional arch in a wall and, in Jaen, the remains of a castle and some Moorish baths. What can be seen instead is some of the finest Renaissance architecture in Spain, largely the work of a genius called Andres de Vandelvira, who was born only a few years after Granada had fallen to the Catholic monarchs in 1492.

Vandelvira was employed for the last thirty years of his life on the cathedral at Jaen, which has been described as only a little smaller than St. Paul's. I would compare it also to Salisbury Cathedral for the unforgettable impression made on first seeing it from afar. The twin towers of Jaen Cathedral, standing majestically against a backdrop of mountains, appear completely to dominate the city.

The Baroque facade was in fact added in the seventeenth century, but the interior is a vision of Renaissance splendour – vast columns, elaborately carved stonework and a wealth of gold above the altar. A coffer, which is not always on display, contains the handkerchief of St Veronica, with which she wiped the face of Christ as he struggled up the hill of Calvary. (Her name is given, in bullfighting, to the first pass made by the matador with his cape.)

The cathedral at Baeza, not many miles to the north-east and across the river Guadalquivir, is also attributed to Vandelvira, though its most unusual feature dates from the early eighteenth century. A hundred-peseta coin placed in a slot in the west wall causes a frescoed screen to slide back, revealing a silver tabernacle about five feet high. Flanked by vases of white roses, it revolves slowly against a red velvet backcloth and the voices of a heavenly choir. The tabernacle is taken out once every year for the procession to celebrate Corpus Christi. (You see some odd things in Spanish cathedrals, none more so than in Santo Domingo de la Calzada, in the north, where a live white cockerel and hen are housed in a wall of the transept.)

Off the cathedral square, other buildings of the same period – a palace, a seminary and the old university – show the influence of Vandelvira, with intricate carving on the facades and attractive loggias

above. One gloriously rich sandstone palace, now the town hall, stands opposite the house where Spain's favourite poet, Antonio Machado, lived for several years after 1912 while teaching at the university. 'Soñare contigo quando no te vea / I will dream of you when I can no longer see you,' he wrote of this exquisite little town. Though born in Seville, Machado spent most of his life outside Andalusia. He is commemorated in Soria and Segovia, where he wrote and taught for some time; and in many other towns streets are named after him.

The crowning glory of the architect Vandelvira is in Ubeda, thanks to an heroic figure who was born there, Francisco de los Cobos. It is easy enough to read 16th-century European history without coming across any reference to Cobos. Yet he was, for some thirty years until his death in 1547, the principal secretary and councillor to the Emperor Charles V.

Cobos did his best to control the imperial budget and restrain the extravagant financial demands of his master, who seemed to be constantly on the move, around Spain and the rest of his Empire. Cobos would often accompany him, and on one occasion in the 1520s they visited Henry VIII's court at Windsor.

In his influential position, Cobos was able to acquire several fortresses around Ubeda and achieved one of his great ambitions, becoming governor of Cazorla and its surrounding sierras, where the source of the River Guadalquivir is to be found. He also enriched himself, mainly by accepting gifts. When a share of Pizarro's treasure from Peru came his way, he decided to employ Vandelvira to build him a lasting memorial in his home town. Work began in 1537 on the chapel of San Salvador: it was to be Cobos's private property, and coats of arms of his and his wife's family were carved on either side of the west door. Cobos was buried there, and the chapel passed, via his daughter-in-law, to the dukes of Medinaceli, who still own it today. The interior has a wonderfully ornate and frescoed dome, and figures from mythology carved on panels.

The imposing facade of the chapel looks over a stone-flagged square, Plaza Vazquez de Molina, which has hardly changed since the 16th century. It has another church on the far side, and two palaces – one, the town hall, with a golden Vandelvira facade, and the other, which is now a *parador*, has a beautifully arched patio, with similar arches repeated on the balcony above. More examples of the architect's work can be found close by – baronial houses richly endowed with loggias and balustrades. And on the outskirts of town Vandelvira designed a hospital: with a grid of quadrangles, it rather resembles Philip II's Escorial near Madrid, which was built at the same time.

While wandering round Ubeda, I came upon a clock tower with a plaque at its base stating that Emperor Charles V visited the town, with his trusted adviser, in 1526. But there is no record of him having returned to see how Cobos and Vandelvira had transformed it. On the same plaque the visit of King Alfonso XIII, with a General Leopoldo Saro, exactly four hundred years later in 1926, is also recorded. In the square opposite, a statue of the general, who fought for Franco in the civil war, is scarred by bullet-holes. It is not known how he died, but in effigy he has been shot four times in the head, twice in the neck and several times in the chest. I felt rather sorry for this little-known military figure, who in later life was given the scarcely dignified title of Conde de la Playa de Ixdain. Who would want to be made count of a beach?

Heading north out of Andalusia, I stopped at a village called Alcaraz, in the foothills of the sierra of that name, with a ruined castle standing on the hill above. I knew nothing about the place, but as I turned into the square there again were the reddish-ochre Renaissance buildings: a corn exchange, an ornate church facade, a palace with a colonnaded loggia, and two grand towers only a few feet apart. Surely the hand of Vandelvira had been at work here? Inquiries established that not only was this so, but that the architect was in fact born in Alcaraz.

It seemed entirely appropriate that Vandelvira's birthplace should be here, at this Iberian watershed – a few miles in one direction from the hills of northern Andalusia, and in another the great stony plains of La Mancha and the country of Don Quixote.

Bibliography

Beevor, Anthony: *The Spanish Civil War* (Orbis, 1982)
Borrow, George: *The Bible in Spain* (Oxford, 1842)
Brenan, Gerald: *The Spanish Labyrinth* (Cambridge, 1943)
       South from Granada (Cambridge, 1957)
Burns, Jimmy: *Spain, A Literary Companion* (John Murray, 1994)
Carr, Raymond: *Spain, 1808–1975* (Oxford, 2nd edition, 1982)
Conrad, Barnaby: *Gates of Fear* (Michael Joseph, 1957)
Ellicott, Dorothy: *Our Gibraltar* (Gibraltar, 1975)
Fergusson, Gordon: *Hounds are Home* (Springwood, 1979)
Fletcher, Ian: *Fields of Fire* (Spellmount, 1994)
Ford, Richard: *Handbook for Travellers in Spain* (John Murray, 1869)
Fraser, Ronald: *Blood of Spain* (Allen Lane, 1979)
Fusi, J. P.: *Franco* (Unwin Hyman, 1987)
Fyrth, Jim: *Women's Voices from the Spanish Civil War* (Lawrence & Wishart, 1991)
Gilmour, David: *The Transformation of Spain* (Quartet, 1985)
       Cities of Spain (John Murray, 1992)
Hare, Augustus: *Wanderings in Spain* (London, 1873)
Hemingway, Ernest: *Death in the Afternoon* (Jonathan Cape, 1932)
       The Dangerous Summer (Hamish Hamilton, 1985)
Hooper, John: *The Spaniards* (Viking, 1986)
Hopkins, Adam: *Spanish Journeys* (Viking, 1992)
Kemp, Peter: *The Thorns of Memory* (Sinclair-Stevenson, 1990)
Keniston, Hayward: *Francisco de los Cobos* (Pittsburgh, 1959)
Longford, Elizabeth: *Wellington – The Years of the Sword* (Weidenfeld & Nicolson, 1969)
Low, Robert: *La Pasionaria* (Hutchinson, 1992)

Luard, Nicholas: *Andalucia* (Century, 1984)

Macaulay, Rose: *Fabled Shore* (Hamish Hamilton, 1949)

Mitchell, Timothy: *Blood Sport* (Pennsylvania, 1991)

Morris, Jan: *Spain* (Faber, 1964)

Morton, H. V.: *A Stranger in Spain* (Methuen, 1955)

Orwell, George: *Homage to Catalonia* (Secker & Warburg, 1938)

Preston, Paul: *Franco* (HarperCollins, 1993)

Pritchett, V. S.: *Marching Spain* (Ernest Benn, 1928)

Quintanilla, Aline: *The Story of Pascualete* (John Murray, 1963)

Scott-Ellis, Priscilla: *The Chances of Death* (Michael Russell, 1995)

Thomas, Hugh: *The Spanish Civil War* (Hamish Hamilton,
    3rd edition, 1977)

Tynan, Kenneth: *Bull Fever* (Harper, 1955)

Vilallonga, Jose Luis de: *The King* (Weidenfeld & Nicolson, 1994)

Wohl, Robert: *The Generation of 1914* (Weidenfeld & Nicolson, 1984)

Index

195

200